The Last Caravaggio

Francesca Whitlum-Cooper

National Gallery Global, London
DISTRIBUTED BY YALE UNIVERSITY PRESS

Published to accompany the exhibition

The Last Caravaggio

The National Gallery, London
18 April–21 July 2024

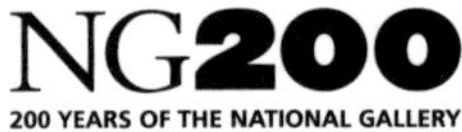

The H J Hyams Exhibition Programme
Supported by The Capricorn Foundation

Exhibition supported by

the
HUO FAMILY
FOUNDATION

This exhibition has been made possible by the provision of insurance through the Government Indemnity Scheme. The National Gallery would like to thank HM Government for providing Government Indemnity and the Department for Culture, Media and Sport and Arts Council England for arranging the indemnity.

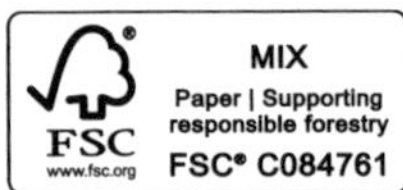

First published in 2024 by
National Gallery Global Limited
Trafalgar Square
London WC2N 5DN
www.shop.nationalgallery.org.uk

ISBN 978 1 85709 720 7
1053470

British Library Cataloguing-in-Publication Data
A catalogue record is available from the British Library
Library of Congress Control Number: 2023951081

PUBLISHER Laura Lappin
PROJECT EDITOR Catherine Hooper
COPY-EDITOR Jenny Wilson
PROOFREADER Robert Davies
PICTURE RESEARCHER Suzanne Bosman
PRODUCTION Jane Hyne

Designed by Philip Lewis
Origination by DL Imaging, London
Printed in Italy by O.G.M.

All works are by Michelangelo Merisi da Caravaggio (1571–1610) unless otherwise stated.
All measurements give height before width.

COVER *The Martyrdom of Saint Ursula*, detail from fig. 1

Contents

Director's Foreword

THE MARTYRDOM OF SAINT URSULA IS CARAVAGGIO'S LAST PAINTING. Within ten weeks of making it, he was dead. Though it was certainly not his intention, the work has taken on the character of a last will and testament. The profound human tragedy it recounts, the dramatic intensity of the storytelling, the powerful deployment of gesture and lighting, and the presence of Caravaggio himself as a witness in the scene, seem to summarise the artist's contribution to the history of art. But, rather amazingly, the painting was practically unknown until 1980.

Painted in Naples for the Genoese nobleman Marcantonio Doria (1572–1651), *The Martyrdom of Saint Ursula* was shipped to Genoa and promptly disappeared from view. It remained with the Dorias in the city until it was taken by a branch of the family in 1832 back to Naples, where it hung unnoticed in the Palazzo Doria d'Angri. By the early twentieth century the painting had passed to the Romana-Avezzano family, who had become the owners of a villa formerly belonging to the Doria d'Angri near Eboli in the province of Salerno. When the painting resurfaced in 1963 in an exhibition in Naples, both the subject matter and the authorship were unrecognised. Ten years later it was acquired by the Neapolitan branch of the Banca Commerciale Italiana (BCI) as a work by Mattia Preti (1613–1699), a painter from Calabria who adopted a Caravaggesque chiaroscuro as part of his style. In 1999 BCI was absorbed into Banca Intesa Sanpaolo, which thereby became the new owner of the painting. It is on public display in the Gallerie d'Italia, on Via Toledo, in an impressive building designed in the Fascist period and recently fully restored and refurbished by Banca Intesa Sanpaolo.

The firm identification of the painting was the work of two Italian art historians, Vincenzo Pacelli (1939–2014) and Ferdinando Bologna (1925–2019). Pacelli had been tipped off by a literary historian, Giorgio Fulco, that there were letters preserved in the state archives in Naples written by Marcantonio Doria's factotum in Naples that referred to a work by Caravaggio. Pacelli transcribed them and teamed up with Bologna, who had studied the BCI painting and had always suspected it was by Caravaggio, to publish an article in the periodical *Prospettiva* in 1980. At a stroke, the entire history of a lost Caravaggio was reconstructed and made known to the public.

I am very grateful to Banca Intesa Sanpaolo for lending the painting for the National Gallery public to enjoy and for supporting the exhibition – the first that takes us into the Gallery's Bicentenary celebrations. Particular thanks are due to Michele Coppola, Executive Director of Art, Culture and Historical Heritage, and curator Antonio Ernesto Denunzio. The Archivio di Stato in Naples has kindly lent one of the Doria letters. This exhibition forms part of the H J Hyams Exhibition Programme, and it is a pleasure to say thank you to the Trustees of the Capricorn Foundation for their ongoing support of the series. I would also like to thank the Huo Family Foundation for their support of this exhibition.

Gabriele Finaldi
DIRECTOR, THE NATIONAL GALLERY

The Last Caravaggio

IN MAY 1610, ONE OF THE MOST INFLUENTIAL PAINTERS OF THE seventeenth century was on the run for the second time in his life. Four years earlier, in May 1606, he had killed a man in Rome and fled south with a *bando capitale* (death warrant) on his head. He travelled first to Naples, and then on to Malta, where, having attained a knighthood, he was thrown into prison for assault. In October 1608, he made a daring escape from this dungeon prison, using rope ladders, the cover of darkness and, presumably, the help of some supporters to haul himself to freedom. Crossing 50 miles of Mediterranean Sea to Sicily, he worked his way from Syracuse to Messina and possibly on to Palermo, enjoying artistic success and receiving major commissions. In Naples, in the autumn of 1609, his enemies finally caught up with him. Stepping out of a tavern, he was viciously wounded on the face 'with such severe slashes that he was almost unrecognisable'.[1] In Rome, where his powerful friends were working to secure him a pardon, it was feared that he had been killed. May 1610 found this artist disgraced, disfigured and ever more desperate to return to Rome. Without knowing it, he was also working on his last painting.

The Martyrdom of Saint Ursula (fig. 1) is the last fully documented painting by Michelangelo Merisi da Caravaggio (1571–1610). It is also the only one of his works for which a contemporary discussion about what would today be called 'painting conservation' survives. Yet until 1974, the painting was not even thought to be by Caravaggio. Attributed to various of his followers, it was only the discovery of two letters (dated 11 and 27 May 1610) in the state archives in Naples that brought the true artist's identity to light (see fig. 6). These letters, confirming the painting's commission in Naples in spring 1610 and detailing its delivery to its patron, the Genoese nobleman Marcantonio Doria (1572–1651), established Caravaggio's authorship.

Today, *The Martyrdom of Saint Ursula* is seen as a quintessential example of Caravaggio's late style. Depicting lifesize figures, its crowded composition is tightly cropped and dramatically lit. Its violence takes place at close quarters. The action unfolds right in front of us, the fatal arrow piercing the saint's chest even as her killer's right hand hangs in the air having just released his bow string. In front of us, too, is Caravaggio himself. For this is not only the artist's last documented painting: it is also his last self portrait (see p. 33). Caravaggio often included his own likeness in his works: his face is a 'constant autobiographical presence in his oeuvre'.[2] Looking over Ursula's shoulder, we see the artist spotlit to the point of deathly pallor (though not, interestingly, disfigured). Pressed in the crush of soldiers, Caravaggio is both participant in the scene and curious witness to it: intimately embroiled in the action but powerless to stop it. The painting captures Ursula in the moments before her martyrdom. Just over two months after it was finished, Caravaggio would be dead too, passing away penniless and alone in the coastal town of Porto Ercole. First charting Caravaggio's meteoric rise to fame and his troubled last years, this book goes on to tell the story of this final painting.

Caravaggio's early life

Caravaggio is one of the most famous artists in the world. He is the subject of books, exhibitions, novels and films. His radically realist style, his painting directly from unidealised live models with dirty feet and grime ingrained in their fingernails, his insistence upon using only one light source that casts powerful light and shadow – this was all new. He had a profound effect on the artists in his own century and continues to do so today. In addition to his paintings, of which there are about 80 or 90, an array of different sources has come down to us about Caravaggio himself. There are the records of the many legal proceedings and accusations made against him, from the capital offence of murder to the act of throwing a plate of artichokes in a waiter's face.[3] There is one detailed description of him by a contemporary – 'a stocky young man … with a thin black beard, thick eyebrows and black eyes, who goes dressed all in black, in a rather disorderly fashion, wearing tattered black hose, and who wears his hair long in the front'[4] – and one drawn portrait that tallies with it (fig. 4). He himself, in a court proceeding, gives us just one line on what he believed a good artist to be: 'one who knows how to paint well and imitate natural objects well'.[5] And there are three detailed seventeenth-century biographies: one written in the late 1610s–early 1620s by Giulio Mancini (1559–1630), a physician who knew Caravaggio in Rome between 1595 and 1600; another published in 1642 by Giovanni Baglione (1566–1643), an artist who had taken Caravaggio to court for writing libellous poems about him; and a third published in 1672 by Giovanni Pietro Bellori (1613–1696), who combined these two earlier sources with detailed research of his own.[6]

Caravaggio's name was not, in fact, Caravaggio. He was born Michelangelo Merisi on 29 September 1571 in Milan, and it was his family's link to the small town of Caravaggio, 25 miles to the east of the city in the fertile plains of Lombardy where he spent much of his childhood, that would lead him to go by his now-famous nickname. His father was a stonemason, while his mother hailed from a family who had links to the powerful Colonna dynasty. The matriarch of this family, Costanza Colonna (about 1556–1626), would support and shelter Caravaggio through some of the darkest periods of his life. His early years were turbulent. His father died when Caravaggio was just six years old, in the middle of an outbreak of bubonic plague that killed a fifth of Milan's population. Throughout the 1570s and 1580s, the city was wracked by pestilence and famine, and governed by the powerful and saintly Archbishop Carlo Borromeo (1538–1584), who believed passionately in the faithful aligning themselves with Christ's suffering. He himself processed barefoot through the city carrying a cross during the height of the plague, and the sermons and candlelit vigils and emphasis on personally feeling Christ's pain must have had some impact on the young Caravaggio. In April 1584, at the age of 13, he was apprenticed to Simone Peterzano (about 1540–1599), a middling painter of frescoes who had trained with Titian. Although this contract stressed that he would 'train in that art night and day' for the next four years, Caravaggio left Peterzano's studio unable to paint in fresco and with almost no traditional artistic training.[7] When he began to paint seriously, he seems to have taught himself.

For a young artist in the seventeenth century, Rome was the ultimate destination: the centre of the Catholic world, a city rich in religious institutions and public commissions, filled with artistic projects and possibilities. Caravaggio arrived in Rome in his early twenties with the energy and enthusiasm of a young man out to make his name. According to Mancini, he was in possession of a 'hot nature and high spirits'; according to Bellori, he was 'disturbed and contentious'.[8] He lived in the dark and dangerous artists' quarter around the Piazza del Popolo and initially struggled to make ends meet. For a time, he lodged with a priest, grumbling so much about being given 'nothing but salad to eat in the evening' that he nicknamed his landlord 'Monsignor Salad'.[9] At another point, he lived with a Sicilian painter 'who had a shop full of crude works of art', for whom he churned out cheap copies.[10] In the studio of Giuseppe Cesari, known as the Cavaliere d'Arpino (1568–1640), he was made to work in the then-nascent and not very highly esteemed genre of still life. Bellori tells us that he 'painted a vase of flowers with the transparencies of the water and glass and the reflections of a window of the room, rendering flowers sprinkled with the freshest dewdrops',[11] describing a picture now lost but bearing a striking resemblance to *Boy bitten by a Lizard* (fig. 7).

Caravaggio yearned to paint figures. His first attempts were strikingly stilted, but the rather stiff *Boy peeling Fruit* (fig. 10) – which may be his earliest surviving picture – was followed by works of increasing sophistication. *Boy with a Basket of Fruit* (fig. 8) and *Sick Bacchus* (fig. 9), both confiscated from the d'Arpino workshop in 1607, were the kinds of works he wanted to be painting while d'Arpino had him painting flowers. The still life in *Boy with a Basket of Fruit* is a brazen advertisement of the artist's skill with a brush. The fruit is painted in exquisite detail, from the bloom of the grapes to the fuzz of the peach to the apple's hard sheen. More than merely turning out a still life, the young Caravaggio was boldly comparing himself to Zeuxis, the Ancient Greek inventor of painting who crafted such realistic grapes that birds would come and peck at them. In the *Sick Bacchus* we meet Caravaggio himself in paint for the first time. Seventeen years and 140 miles from that last Neapolitan self portrait, he painted himself here with a similarly sickly pallor (he may have been recovering from an illness that landed him in Rome's Ospedale della Consolazione [Hospital of the Consolation]). Unable to afford a model, he painted his own likeness using a mirror: in 1605, when Caravaggio failed to pay his bills and his landlady seized his possessions, a mirror was listed among his belongings.[12]

These early figure paintings had a considerable impact. The German artist and writer Joachim von Sandrart (1606–1688), who visited Rome in the 1630s, later recalled *Boy bitten by a Lizard*: 'it is marvellous to look at and it caused [Caravaggio's] reputation to increase notably throughout Rome'.[13] Even the jealous Baglione had to admit that 'it was all done meticulously … you could almost hear the boy scream'.[14] Caravaggio was later quoted as saying that painting flowers required as much artistry as painting figures.[15] Caravaggio had arrived in the city with little formal training and no real connections, but he was resilient and resourceful. Even as he worked in other painters' studios – he spent time in the workshop of Antiveduto Grammatica (1571–1626) as well as the Cavaliere d'Arpino's – he made use of Rome's emerging network of picture-dealers, some of whom specialised in selling artworks and others of whom, perhaps barbers and tailors by trade, did so on the side. One picture-dealer, a certain Constantino Spata who had a shop near the church of San Luigi dei Francesi, would play a pivotal role in Caravaggio's fortunes. It was through Spata that Caravaggio met Francesco Maria del Monte (1549–1627), a Roman cardinal and connoisseur with a penchant for card-playing,[16] the man who was going to change his life.

The Fortune Teller and *The Cardsharps* took the tricksters of everyday Rome and transposed them to canvas. Against a sandy background, a beautiful gypsy, her hair swept up in a white scarf, reads the palm of a rich young man (fig. 11). The feathered plume of his hat flutters in the breeze; the hilt of his sword catches the light, as does the silky brocade of his suit. So entranced is he by the woman's smile that he fails to notice as she slides the gold ring off his finger. In another painting of deception, two young men play cards (fig. 12). The wealthy youth in black considers his cards so carefully that he does not see the bystander revealing his hand to his opponent, who is ready to pull the winning card – either of hearts or clubs – from his belt. No one had painted anything like this before. Cardinal del Monte was entranced, buying the paintings and offering Caravaggio lodgings in his palazzo. Unlike those of his painted dupes in their finery and feathered hats, the artist's fortunes were looking up.[17]

Roman success

In the autumn of 1595, Caravaggio moved into the Palazzo Madama, one of Cardinal del Monte's two imposing Roman residences. He was given 'an honoured place' in the cardinal's household, which – far from the gritty, grimy streets Caravaggio was used to – must have been a riot of colour and sound.[18] Del Monte was a Renaissance man, a lover of painting, sculpture, music and science, and his palazzo was filled with everything from precious stones and antique sculptures to a telescope given to him by Galileo.[19] Caravaggio thrived and was soon commissioned by the cardinal to paint a picture that epitomises the heady atmosphere of del Monte's household. In *The Musicians* (fig. 13), three young men in antique dress and a winged Cupid prepare to perform. The central figure tunes his lute; on the right, with his back to us, a singer rehearses his lines. The lutenist may be a portrait of a castrato in the cardinal's retinue, for there is at least one other portrait in the painting. In the background on the right, Caravaggio himself has assumed the role of cornetto-player, his flushed cheeks the picture of health compared to that sallow Bacchus. Baglione tells us that Caravaggio 'was given room and board' by del Monte, 'and soon he felt stimulated and confident'.[20] This self portrait would seem to confirm that.

Caravaggio had every reason to feel confident. Protected and promoted by del Monte, he grew steadily more famous, and soon he was painting for the great and the good of Rome. For the banker and art collector Vincenzo Giustiniani (1564–1637) he painted another lute-player, a sultry, round-faced castrato, where 'everything seemed lively and real' (fig. 14).[21] For Cardinal Federico Borromeo (1564–1631), cousin of the Archbishop of Milan, he painted his only pure still life, a basket of fruit that simultaneously blooms and decays before us. He also produced a handful of portraits and several pictures for private devotion, supposedly picking his models off the street. There is *The Penitent Magdalene* (fig. 16), where a red-headed Roman girl sits folded low on a chair, her cast-off jewels beside her, so real and ordinary that Bellori described her as 'a girl drying her hair ... pretending that she is the Magdalen'.[22] For del Monte again, there was *Saint Catherine of Alexandria* (fig. 17), for which the well-known local courtesan Fillide Melandroni (1581–1618) modelled as the martyr saint. Counter to the centuries-old impulse to make art elegant and beautiful, Caravaggio made 'no attempt to improve on the creations of Nature'.[23] For his supporters, the emphatic naturalism of these paintings – their everyday figures, their earthy colours, their strong lighting always from above and from a single source – was intoxicating.

Yet for all this success among Rome's private patrons, Caravaggio was desperate to win a public commission: that is, the chance to have a large-scale painting in a church where the whole of Rome, rather than a few invited guests, could see his work. In July 1599, with del Monte's help, he got his chance. The church of San Luigi dei Francesi was a stone's throw from the Palazzo Madama, and its priests needed two paintings on the life of Saint Matthew for the burial chapel of French cardinal Matthieu Cointerel (in Italian, Matteo Contarelli, 1519–1585) (fig. 15). For the first time in his life, Caravaggio had to paint not one but two monumental paintings: at some 322 cm tall by 340 cm wide, these were three times the size of anything he had worked on before and would end up incorporating four times as many figures.

In *The Calling of Saint Matthew*, Caravaggio's Christ walks into a dingy room in contemporary Rome (fig. 18). Matthew, the tax collector, sits at a bare table surrounded by young boys counting coins and an old man adjusting his glasses. He points at his chest, as if unable to believe that Christ – whose outstretched hand copies the hand of God in Michelangelo's Sistine Chapel – has come for him. The single shaft of light is both the echo of the daylight falling from the chapel's window onto the canvas and the light of God. Across the chapel, *The Martyrdom of Saint Matthew* came less easily to Caravaggio, who had to paint it twice (fig. 19). Again, the New Testament has been brought up to the present day. The rich colours of his earlier paintings have become more 'boldly dark and black', the lighting even more exaggerated in the service of volume.[24] And once again, Caravaggio himself appears, his face glimpsed in the figure of a background onlooker – both a visual signature establishing his authorship by painting himself into the scene, and a tacit admission that he, like those around him, would not have been brave enough to stay the executioner's sword.

These paintings made Caravaggio famous, but they were not universally admired. All three contemporary biographers wrestle with the immediate impact these works had on artists in Rome. According to Bellori, 'the young ones particularly gathered around him, praised him as the unique imitator of nature, and looked on his work as miracles ... [outdoing] each other in imitating his works ... [w]ithout devoting themselves to study and instruction'.[25] There was undoubtedly admiration for Caravaggio's innovations, but the art world has often been resistant to change. In painting figures from the life, who were so drastically unidealised, Caravaggio was turning his back on a centuries-old tradition in which it was the artist's role to idealise the world around him.[26] In comparison with the works of Raphael (1483–1520) and Michelangelo (1475–1564), Caravaggio's extreme fidelity to the world around him was seen by contemporaries as mechanical, uninformed and even unworthy. Caravaggio's paintings for the Contarelli Chapel were revolutionary. But despite the fact that they unleashed a pictorial revolution that spread throughout Western Europe, from the Utrecht *Caravaggisti* such as Gerrit van Honthorst (1592–1656) and Hendrick ter Brugghen (1588–1629) in the north to the Spaniards Jusepe de Ribera (1591–1652) and Francisco de Zurbarán

(1598–1664) in the south, they went against everything the art world stood for, and the discomfort they caused goes a long way to explaining why Caravaggio was largely forgotten in the eighteenth and nineteenth centuries.[27]

By 1601, Caravaggio had moved from del Monte's palazzo into that of the Mattei brothers – three noblemen who formed one of the greatest Roman art collections. For the Mattei he would paint *The Supper at Emmaus* (fig. 21), startling his contemporaries with his depiction of the unbearded Christ in a Roman tavern, capturing the very moment at which his disciples recognise him. With arms outstretched and a ragged elbow jutting out of the canvas towards us, we are flung into the action. This picture's pendant, *The Taking of Christ* (fig. 20) – considered lost for centuries until it was discovered in a Jesuit refectory in Dublin in 1990 – likewise catapults us into the heartbreaking moment of Christ's betrayal. The canvas is a whirl of drapery, a riot of tightly packed figures and menacingly glinting armour, over which Caravaggio watches, again a bystander at the crossroads of good and evil. Christ's anguished hands stretch towards us, as if we could touch them.

As the seventeenth century got underway, Caravaggio's supporters continued to champion him. He had a few church commissions under his belt. But his paintings were getting darker, both literally and figuratively. His naturalism grew more extreme. If the Roman church could stomach the ragged clothes and filthy feet of the pilgrims kneeling before the Virgin in *The Madonna of Loreto* (fig. 22), other paintings could not be tolerated. A third painting of Saint Matthew, intended as the altarpiece for the Contarelli Chapel, had to be repainted and replaced, having 'neither decorum nor the appearance of a saint'.[28] The *Madonna and Child with Saint Anne* hung for two days in the parish church of the Vatican, for which it had been commissioned, before being removed: the Virgin's buxom chest was 'offensive' and not the stuff of altarpieces (fig. 23).[29] Most celebrated of all these refusals is *The Death of the Virgin* (fig. 24), whose mother of Christ, barefoot and swollen-bellied, was, in Mancini's words, modelled by 'some dirty prostitute from the Ortaccio',[30] Rome's red-light district. Caravaggio's realism was getting him into increasingly hotter water.

The backdrop to these professional successes and disappointments was a life growing ever more violent and disturbed. What had begun in May 1598 with his arrest for carrying a sword – which Caravaggio maintained he had the right to do, being a member of del Monte's household – now escalated into an almost back-to-back litany of charges against him.[31] In September 1603, he was on trial for penning abusive poems about Baglione, his future biographer. 1604 saw three arrests: for smashing a plate of artichokes in a waiter's face, throwing stones at the police and verbally abusing a police officer. Twice in 1605 he was arrested for hurling abuse or physical objects at the home of someone who had offended him, as well as being taken into custody for committing serious assault and being injured in a fight. In May 1606, things came to a head when he killed a long-time enemy, the pimp Ranuccio Tomassoni, in a swordfight. His Roman protectors could do nothing for him now: Caravaggio was on the run.

Exile: Naples, Malta and Sicily

After Tomassoni bled to death on a tennis court, Caravaggio was a wanted man with a *bando capitale* on his head. This meant that any person in the Papal States had the right to kill him and produce his severed head as evidence. This punishment loomed heavily over Caravaggio, who later used his own self portrait for the giant Goliath's severed head (fig. 25). He got out of Rome quickly, making first for the Alban Hills, about 12 miles south-east of Rome, and then for the town of Zagarolo, where he found protection with his old friends, the Colonna family. Here he painted a second version of *The Supper at Emmaus* (fig. 26). It is hard not to read some of the artist's despair in this darker, more claustrophobic iteration, with its careworn, wrinkled faces, its muted palette, its impenetrable black background.[32] Selling this version may have paid for Caravaggio's onward journey to Naples, another city in which he could enjoy the Colonnas' protection.

Seventeenth-century Naples was part of the Spanish Empire and ruled by a Spanish viceroy, beyond the reaches of the Papal

States and their *bando capitale*. It was a city of contrasts: at once the largest metropolis in Italy with vast wealth brought in by its port, but also dark, dirty and overcrowded with a quarter of a million people of all nationalities squeezed into a narrow warren of streets. It would have a profound impact on Caravaggio's art, and vice versa: away from the traditions and hierarchies of Rome, Caravaggio was enormously successful and even more influential.[33] Nowhere is Naples itself glimpsed more clearly in Caravaggio's work than in the masterpiece of his first stay in the city, *The Seven Acts of Mercy* (fig. 27), which was commissioned for the church of Pio Monte della Misericordia in the autumn of 1606. In this one monumental canvas, the seven acts of Christian mercy – bury the dead, visit the imprisoned, feed the hungry, shelter the homeless, clothe the naked, visit the sick and refresh the thirsty – are crammed into one Neapolitan street corner. Even as the woman at right gives milk to the prisoner, we see the feet of a corpse being carried off for burial. In the background, a man drinks from the jawbone of an ass while the seated beggar receives a cut of the cloak of the young man before him. Over it all hover the Virgin and Child and two angels, encircled by a curiously static tumult of feather and fabric. Other commissions followed, but while Naples was hungry for Caravaggio's art, he felt the need to continue onward. Whether spurred by ambition or fear or both, in June 1607 he set sail for Malta on a flotilla captained by Fabrizio Sforza Colonna (1580–1625), his old protectress Costanza Colonna's son.

If Naples was dark and unruly, Malta was strictly ordered, a rocky island fortress ruled by the Knights of Saint John, an elite religious fighting force charged with protecting pilgrims on their way to the Holy Land. Caravaggio landed in Valletta with the intention of joining the Order of Saint John: this would not only help in his pleas for a pardon from Rome, but also ensure that he returned to the Eternal City with glory. The Grand Master of the Order, Alof de Wignacourt (1547–1622), accepted his candidacy, commissioning two portraits of himself in his full regalia (see fig. 29). During the year as a novice before he was able to fully enter the brotherhood, Caravaggio also painted a vast altarpiece of the Order's patron saint for St John's Co-Cathedral, in which he put 'all the force of his brush to use' (fig. 28).[34] Across more than five metres of canvas, Caravaggio depicted the very moment of Saint John's execution, as bleak as it is brutal. Blood spurts from the Baptist's neck as the muscled executioner reaches for his knife a second time to finish the job. The elderly female witness clasps her face; Salome, lowering the golden platter on which she will parade the severed head, seems overcome by the weight of the object and the moment. All the figures are dwarfed by the formidable prison architecture, its dangling ropes a curious foreshadowing of the artist's own imprisonment on Malta. Famously, he signs his name in the saint's blood – *f. michelangelo* – confidently adding the 'f.' (*fra*) to signify his elevation to the brotherhood.[35] But he was too eager. Although he officially joined the Order on 14 July 1608 as a *cavaliere di Obbedienza*, just six weeks later he was thrown into a dungeon cell for 'an ill-considered quarrel with a noble knight'.[36] His flight from this prison cell and from Malta, against all the Order's rules, meant that he was derobed *in absentia* and on the run again.

From Malta Caravaggio reached Sicily, where he spent a semi-itinerant year. Although he reconnected with an old friend – the minor painter Mario Minniti (1577–1640), who had posed for some of his early Roman pictures (see fig. 8) – and found commissions, such as the austere but deeply affecting *Burial of Saint Lucy* for the Syracusan church of Santa Lucia al Sepolcro, he must have been continually looking over his shoulder. From Syracuse he made his way to Messina and then perhaps on to Palermo. By the autumn of 1609 he was back in Naples. There was still huge demand for his paintings here. With a severely restricted palette and impenetrable dark background, Caravaggio depicts Salome receiving the head of John the Baptist (fig. 30) with extraordinary economy of means, both at a compositional level and in his abbreviated strokes of paint. He captures the story in a moment of suspension – literally, in terms of the head being placed on the salver, but figuratively, too, as each character responds to the violence in front of them: the resolve of the brutish executioner, the old woman's quiet contemplation, Salome's look of either shame or disgust. The formal echoes across the canvas emphasise the painting's intense psychological power: Salome and the executioner incline their heads at the same angle, just as the old woman's tilted head mirrors that of the Baptist. Nonetheless there is a sense that, despite their proximity, each figure is utterly isolated.

In late 1609, Caravaggio's enemies finally caught up with him. He was leaving a tavern when he was surrounded and slashed on the face – perhaps by the 'noble knight' seeking revenge for his own attack on Malta. Seriously wounded, Caravaggio was confined for several months to the house of Costanza Colonna in Chiaia, a wealthy waterfront neighbourhood on the western side of Naples. When he was well enough, sometime in the spring of 1610, it was *The Martyrdom of Saint Ursula* (fig. 1) to which he turned.

The Martyrdom of Saint Ursula

On 11 May 1610 a man named Lanfranco Massa sat down in Naples to write a letter to his employer in Genoa (fig. 6). The letter was addressed to the Genoese nobleman Marcantonio Doria, Prince of Angri and later Duke of Eboli, for whom Massa acted as business agent in Naples, and it concerned a painting that Doria had recently commissioned from the most celebrated artist then working in the southern city. The letter's discovery in 1980 by the art historian Vincenzo Pacelli had a profound impact not only on our understanding of Caravaggio's last period but also on the painting in question, which until then was not so much the *last* Caravaggio as a *lost* Caravaggio. Massa wrote:

> I had intended to send you the picture of Saint Ursula this week, but to make sure of sending it perfectly dry I put it out yesterday in the sun, which, rather than drying out the varnish, made it soften, since Caravaggio applied it quite thickly; I will go round to said Caravaggio's again to get his opinion on what to do so I can be sure of not ruining it; Signor Damiano has seen it, and was amazed, like everyone else who has seen it.[37]

Prior to the discovery of this letter in the archives, opinion was divided on *The Martyrdom of Saint Ursula*, which belonged to the Banca Commerciale Italiana. Several scholars including Roberto Longhi – perhaps the most influential art historian working on Caravaggio in the twentieth century – thought it to be by Bartolomeo Manfredi (1582–1622), a Roman contemporary who played a major role in the diffusion of Caravaggio's innovations.[38] Others thought it to be by Mattia Preti (1613–1699), a Calabrian painter a generation younger than Caravaggio who had been deeply marked by his style.[39] Since the mid-1970s, art historian Mina Gregori had been suggesting the painting was by Caravaggio's hand, but the letters provided the crucial link.[40] The attribution was strengthened by the discovery of two seventeenth-century inscriptions on the back of the original canvas: one, albeit giving an impossible date, reads *D. Michel Angelo da / Caravagio* [sic] *1616* and the other gives the initials *M. A. D.* surmounted by a cross, which would have been written after the death in 1651 of Marcantonio Doria (fig. 5). The rediscovery of the letter among the Doria papers in the state archives in Naples and the connection it made to the Doria family means that *The Martyrdom of Saint Ursula*'s full history can now be traced from the moment it left Caravaggio's studio right up to the present day. In identifying the painting as the last documented work by Caravaggio's hand, it also gives us the opportunity to look closely at his art in what would turn out to be the final months of his life.

Today, *The Martyrdom of Saint Ursula* is in a somewhat compromised condition. Whatever damage Massa caused by setting the painting out in the Neapolitan sun to dry was worsened by its return journey to Naples in 1832, when the packing materials adhered to the painting's surface, and by harsh historic restorations.[41] Yet the painting continues to reveal its secrets: it was not until the conservation treatment of 2004 that the bystander's hand, previously covered by overpaint, was revealed (fig. 3), returning the full dramatic intensity to the composition.[42] Some art historians, knowing the circumstances of Caravaggio's second visit to Naples – the violent attack, his long convalescence – have read into his final paintings 'an uncontrollable shaking of the hands, as well as perhaps ... damage to the eyes'.[43] Others, even more perceptively, have seen 'conscious aesthetic and practical distinctions' being made.[44] In *The Denial of Saint Peter* (fig. 31), for example, which was painted speculatively for the open market, Caravaggio's brushwork is highly abbreviated, the woman's headscarf and the folds of the saint's sleeves created out of a handful of bold, loose strokes. *The Martyrdom of Saint Ursula*, by contrast, reveals a much more considered application of paint, befitting a significant commission from a major patron. The brilliant sheen of the Hun's silver armour is created by applying white paint in two different, almost cross-hatched directions, while its flourish of gold decoration is built up from dark and mid tones to the brilliant white gleam of its highlight (fig. 2). The armour at the right-hand edge of the canvas, with its menacingly glinting jointed sleeve, is similarly detailed, even down to the gold studs that hold it together, while Ursula's gown – albeit damaged – reveals details of delicate gold embroidery indicative of the care and attention Caravaggio gave to this canvas. Although these two paintings were made with a very different approach and for different circumstances, it is fascinating to note the re-use of the same sixteenth-century helmet, which Caravaggio must have had in his studio.[45]

A second letter with annotations in its margins reveals that Massa put *The Martyrdom of Saint Ursula* on a boat on 27 May 1610 and that it arrived in Genoa on 18 June.[46] It remained there until 1832, returning to Naples in the collection of a Doria descendant, and was acquired by the Banca Commerciale – as a work by Preti – in 1973. Marcantonio Doria already knew Caravaggio when *The Martyrdom of Saint Ursula* was commissioned: Massa's letter of 11 May 1610 includes a reference to another potential painting from Caravaggio, 'whom I know to be a friend of Your Grace's'.[47] They would have met in Genoa in 1605, when Caravaggio fled Rome following two charges of defacing doors and one of assault. Almost exclusively religious in tone, dominated by the Neapolitan school and mostly depicting single figures or small groups, Doria's collection of paintings was characterised by a realism that was inspired by Caravaggio's innovative style and which spoke to

Doria's strong Christian faith. The commission of *The Martyrdom of Saint Ursula* from Caravaggio himself has been described as the 'culmination' of his collecting efforts.[48] Caravaggio's return to Naples was a chance for Doria not only to buy a major work from a great artist, but also to commission one with a deeply personal connection. His stepdaughter, Livia Grimaldi, was at this time professing as a nun in the Trinità delle Monache convent in Naples and had taken the name 'Sister Ursula'. Letters sent from Naples to Doria in Genoa throughout 1608 allude to the difficult time Livia was having within the religious order.[49] Doria's sympathies with his stepdaughter probably account for his unusual choice of subject matter in asking Caravaggio to depict Saint Ursula.

The most popular account of Ursula's life comes from *The Golden Legend*, a collection of more than 150 lives of the saints written by Jacobus de Voragine in 1265 and read widely throughout early modern Europe. According to *The Golden Legend*, Ursula was a British or Breton Christian princess whose hand in marriage was sought by Ethereus, Prince of Anglia. Seeking to defer her marriage and thus preserve her virginity – a common motif in early Christianity – Ursula asked her suitor to send her ten virgins, and a thousand virgins to each of them, and to be baptised and to give her 'space of three years to dedicate her virginity'.[50] The prince, a willing convert to Christianity, agreed, and Ursula and her virgin followers – some light confusion in the calculations has led to this figure being written as 11,000 – set sail for the port of Tielle (present-day Tiel), in the Netherlands. The legend recounts that they travelled to Cologne and then on to Rome. It was on their return to Cologne that the Huns massacred Ursula's followers. Seeing Ursula, however, the Prince of the Huns was so struck by her beauty that he offered to save her life by marrying her. When she refused, 'he shot at her an arrow, and pierced her through the body, and so accomplished her martyrdom'.[51]

When tasked with depicting Ursula and the story of her martyrdom, other artists over the centuries had tended to focus on quantity. One strand of iconography showed Ursula physically sheltering her virgin followers beneath her cloak: this can be seen on a rather naïve 'Ursula shrine' in Bruges (fig. 34), and on the much more finely and beautifully painted example of a shrine containing the saint's relics decorated by Hans Memling (active 1465; died 1494) (fig. 35). Another artistic impulse was towards the chaos of a battlefield strewn with virgins, as in Vittore Carpaccio's (1465–1525) *Martyrdom of the Pilgrims and Funeral of Saint Ursula* for the Scuola di Sant'Orsola in Venice (fig. 33). Closer to Caravaggio's time, Ludovico Carracci (1555–1619) had painted Ursula as a visionary, calm amidst the tumult of massacre (fig. 32), for the church of San Nicolò e San Domenico in Imola. While Caravaggio had certainly shown that he could paint tumult – in *The Martyrdom of Saint Matthew* (fig. 19), for example – Marcantonio Doria's commission was for a private painting, not a public altarpiece. Caravaggio's treatment of the subject was to some extent conditioned by the size of the work that was being asked of him, yet it played to his strengths. Painting half-length, lifesize figures who stood in close proximity to the viewer steered him towards a much more intimate and disturbing depiction of the saint.

In a 1620 inventory of Doria paintings in Genoa, Caravaggio's *Martyrdom of Saint Ursula* was described as 'Saint Ursula stabbed by the tyrant', which is exactly what we see in the painting.[52] With typical intensity and clarity of narrative vision, Caravaggio has eschewed the mass murder of the accompanying virgins, condensing the legend's plot to its key actors. The action takes place in a tent: swathes of fabric act as backdrop, creating a claustrophobic space, with Caravaggio's typical single light source illuminating the figures from the left. As our eye moves across the canvas, the action unfolds almost cinematically. Film director Martin Scorsese could have been describing this painting when he said, of Caravaggio's works, 'You sort of come upon the scene midway and you're immersed in it.'[53] There is the Hun, with his deeply lined face and glinting armour, his expression capturing both fury and regret. There is the shadowy figure of the bystander, too late to stop him. There is Ursula, transfixed both literally and figuratively by the arrow in her breast. And then the soldiers, frozen in horror, as if even they cannot believe what has happened. The composition is a moment of stillness, absorption, a freeze-frame in which each figure must reckon with and account for their role in what has happened. This sense of a group of people bearing witness to an atrocity packs an extreme psychological punch. The varied expressions are matched by an intricate play of hands across the canvas: the guilty hands of the Hun having just fired the fatal arrow; the desperate hand of the bystander trying to interject; and Ursula's already pale fingers framing the wound in her chest. The artist permits no extraneous detail in his composition. We enter the narrative at its most difficult and emotionally charged point.

At the heart of the painting is Ursula herself. What are we to make of her expression here? She manages to look both surprised and serene; accepting of this fatal wound, even as her brow furrows, even as she feels the injury out with her fingers. For someone so intent on preserving her virginity, the penetration of the Hun's arrow has an unavoidably sexual connotation, one emphasised here by Caravaggio's placement of her hands and the blood spurting from the wound. This scene is dominated by men, its violence explicitly masculine. Unlike earlier depictions, with their focus on Ursula's thousands of virginal followers, Caravaggio casts the saint as a lone female presence. She is at once both isolated within this male space and surrounded by the press of its soldiers. This effect would surely be heightened were we to see the painting in its original condition, for in its present state of conservation it is easy to read the scene as one containing just five figures and to overlook the soldier wearing the helmet that appears beyond Ursula's head and the shadowy figure between the Hun and the bystander. Massa's letter to Doria tells us that everyone who saw the painting in Naples was amazed. Was it the innovative composition that drew their admiration, or the condensed drama, or the emotional pitch, or the overall effect? Could it have been this pale, pensive Ursula, painted as both heroine and victim, sharing her final moments with the viewer in such uncomfortably close quarters?

The Martyrdom of Saint Ursula is undeniably a scene of violence and aggression, yet, according to her legend, this was a fate that Ursula actively chose. However atrocious, her death was the price she was willing to pay for her faith. This sense of autonomy – the idea that Ursula had chosen faith over life – was something for which she was celebrated in the Middle Ages, certainly by women.

Although the origin of the legend and its historical veracity remain murky, Ursula has always been a very popular figure. In the twelfth century, a mass grave was discovered beneath a church in Cologne and quickly identified with the remains of Ursula and her 11,000 followers.[54] This association was crystallised by the revelations of the mystic Elisabeth von Schönau (about 1129–1164), which became hugely famous, and the bones were venerated as relics across Europe. Many were used to decorate the walls of the Golden Chamber of the Basilica of St Ursula in Cologne itself (fig. 37); others were placed into sculpted reliquary busts, several of which have hollow relic compartments in the figure's breast exactly where Caravaggio would later place the focus of his painting (fig. 36).[55] In Caravaggio's native Lombardy, Angela de Merici (1474–1540) founded the Order of the Ursulines with a mission to honour Saint Ursula and educate young women. Although questions about the historicity of the saint's legend saw the Roman Catholic Church remove her feast day from the liturgical calendar in 1969, Ursula continues to be seen as a figurehead for faith, devotion and female empowerment. However pale she is in Caravaggio's depiction, however close we are to her final moments, Ursula does not crumble. Perhaps it was this courageous Ursula that Livia Grimaldi sought to emulate as she took her vows in Naples, and whom her stepfather wanted to commemorate by commissioning this painting.

The last months

Peering over others at the martyr saint's murder, as he had at Christ's betrayal eight years before (see figs 1 and 20), Caravaggio paints himself here pale and powerless. This is our last glimpse of a desperate man emerging from one of the most troubled moments of his life. Yet as dire as his circumstances must have seemed as he lay convalescing from his attack in Naples, Caravaggio had reason to be hopeful. His powerful friends in Rome had continued to campaign for his pardon, and the possibility of returning to the Eternal City was now closer than ever. Unlike in *The Taking of Christ*, where his sight is firmly fixed on the moment of Christ's capture,

Caravaggio seems in *The Martyrdom of Saint Ursula* to look beyond the picture's edge, as if even while painting it he was looking to his next steps. The painting sailed from Naples for Genoa on 27 May 1610 and, just six weeks later, Caravaggio followed. Believing that a papal pardon had finally been granted, he boarded a *felucca* (sailing boat) and headed for Rome.[56]

What happened next has been the subject of much debate, but the early sources tell us that when Caravaggio came ashore at Palo (the port closest to Rome) he was arrested by mistake and separated from his belongings.[57] The *felucca*, carrying everything he owned and, crucially, three of his paintings, continued to sail north up the coast to the town of Porto Ercole. Both Baglione and Bellori describe the artist '[running] along the beach in the heat of the summer sun', 'trying to catch sight of the vessel that had his belongings'.[58] While this must be dramatic licence – Caravaggio could not have tried running 70 miles on foot – both biographers nevertheless vividly capture his horror and desperation. Arriving in Spanish-controlled Porto Ercole, Caravaggio, who was probably still weakened from the Neapolitan attack, sank into a 'malignant fever' and 'died as miserably as he had lived'.[59] It was an inglorious end for someone whose oeuvre includes some of the most powerful works of art ever painted. Bellori captures the sorrow felt by Caravaggio's friends in Rome who, even as the news of his death arrived, 'were waiting enthusiastically for his return'.[60] He quotes a poem written by Caravaggio's close friend, the poet Giambattista Marino (1569–1625), for the occasion of his funeral:

> Death and Nature made a cruel plot against you, Michele:
> Nature was afraid
> Your hand would surpass it in every image:
> You created, not painted.[61]

Brawling, duelling, murdering and fleeing, Caravaggio might not have been able to tame his own nature, but the consensus of his contemporaries – and many of those who look at his paintings today – was that he painted the world around him like no other.

Notes

1 Baglione 1642, in Langdon 2016, p. 57.
2 Vodret 2010, cat. 64, p. 208.
3 For a comprehensive account of the documents relating to Caravaggio, including his various trials and misdemeanours, see Macioce 2023.
4 Corradini and Marini 1998, p. 27.
5 Dell'Acqua and Cinotti 1971, pp. 153–7.
6 Though they do not always tally, these three biographies are invaluable sources on Caravaggio's life, and can be consulted in English in Langdon 2016.
7 For Caravaggio's apprenticeship contract, see Macioce 2023, Doc. 279*, pp. 49–50. For a concise discussion of Caravaggio's technique across the early, middle and late paintings at the National Gallery, see Keith 1998. A broader discussion of technique across the artist's oeuvre can be found in Milan 2017–18.
8 Mancini 1617–21, in Langdon 2016, p. 31; Bellori 1672, in Langdon 2016, p. 63.
9 Mancini 1617–21, in Langdon 2016, p. 31.
10 Baglione 1642, in Langdon 2016, p. 45.
11 Bellori 1672, in Langdon 2016, p. 64.
12 Macioce 2023, Doc. 651*, pp. 204–5.
13 Sandrart 1675, p. 189.
14 Baglione 1642, in Langdon 2016, p. 45.
15 Vincenzo Giustiniani to Dirk van Ameyden, about 1620, in Enggass and Brown 1970, p. 17.
16 Enggass and Brown 1970, p. 17.
17 For more on Caravaggio's cardsharps, see Spear 2020.
18 Bellori 1672, in Langdon 2016, p. 68. For more on the artistic environment of seventeenth-century Rome, see Cavazzini 2008, Milan and Paris 2014, and Paris 2018–19.
19 For more about Caravaggio's relationship with Cardinal del Monte, see Spezzaferro 1971 and Gilbert 1995.
20 Baglione 1642, in Langdon 2016, p. 46.
21 Ibid.
22 Bellori 1672, in Langdon 2016, p. 66.
23 Ibid.
24 Ibid., p. 71.
25 Ibid., p. 72.
26 For the innovation of painting from real models, see Christiansen 1986.
27 For more on Caravaggio's influence and posthumous reputation see Cleveland 1971 and London, Dublin and Edinburgh 2016–17.
28 Bellori 1672, in Langdon 2016, p. 73.
29 Ibid., p. 101.
30 Mancini 1617–21, in Langdon 2016, p. 39.
31 See Macioce 2023.
32 For a survey of Caravaggio's final years, see London 2005.
33 For an overview of painting in seventeenth-century Naples, see London 1982 and Spinosa 2010. For Caravaggio in Naples, see Terzaghi in Naples 2019, pp. 30–60.
34 Bellori 1672, in Langdon 2016, p. 91.
35 For more on Caravaggio on Malta, see Valletta (Malta) 2007 and Sciberras 2023.

36 Bellori 1672, in Langdon 2016, p. 91.
37 Archivio Doria d'Angri, in the Archivio di Stato di Napoli, parte II, b290, reproduced (in the original Italian) in Pacelli and Bologna 1980, p. 24.
38 See F. Bologna in London 2005, cat. 144, p. 146.
39 See Naples 1963, cat. 50, p. 36, and F. Bologna in London 2005, cat. 144, p. 146.
40 See M. Gregori in Rome, Milan and Vicenza 2004, pp. 48–55.
41 For full conservation history, see Pagano in Rome, Milan and Vicenza 2004, pp. 90–9, and for the 1832 incident p. 95.
42 Ibid., p. 97.
43 Graham-Dixon 2010, p. 421.
44 Christiansen 2019, p. 37.
45 The same helmet later appears in Battistello Caracciolo's *The Liberation of Saint Peter* (1615, Pio Monte della Misericordia, Naples), suggesting it continued to serve as a prop in Neapolitan studios after Caravaggio's departure. See Christiansen 2019, p. 35.
46 See Pacelli and Bologna 1980, pp. 24–5 and footnote 9.
47 Ibid. (in the original Italian), p. 24.
48 Santamaria 2019, see pp. 118–21 in particular.
49 See A. Denunzio in Naples 2014–15, cat. 15, pp. 138–40.
50 Jacobus de Voragine, *The Golden Legend* [*Aurea Legenda*], 1275, trans. William Caxton, 1483, vol. 6, pp. 30 ff: https://sourcebooks.fordham.edu/basis/goldenlegend/GoldenLegend-Volume6.asp#Eleven%20Thousand%20Virgins [accessed October 2023].
51 Ibid.
52 See A. Denunzio in Milan 2017–18, pp. 190–3.
53 Quoted in Graham-Dixon 2010, p. 441.
54 Cusack 1999, pp. 101–2.
55 With grateful thanks to Siobhán Jolley for pointing me in this direction and for all her guidance on Saint Ursula.
56 For a contemporary reference to the papal pardon having been granted, see Macioce 2023, Doc. 890*, p. 285.
57 Baglione 1642, in Langdon 2016, p. 57; Bellori 1672, in Langdon 2016, p. 95.
58 Bellori 1672, in Langdon 2016, p. 95; Baglione 1642, in Langdon 2016, p. 57.
59 Bellori 1672, in Langdon 2016, p. 95; Baglione 1642, in Langdon 2016, p. 60.
60 Bellori 1672, in Langdon 2016, p. 95.
61 Ibid.

Bibliography

CAVAZZINI 2008
P. Cavazzini, *Painting as Business in Early Seventeenth-Century Rome*, University Park, PA 2008

CHRISTIANSEN 1986
K. Christiansen, 'Caravaggio and "L'esempio davanti del naturale"', *The Art Bulletin*, 68, no. 3 (1986), pp. 421–45

CHRISTIANSEN 2019
K. Christiansen, 'Some Thoughts on Caravaggio, the Market, Style, and Chronology', in F. Baldassari and M. Confalone (eds), *Gli amici per Nicola Spinosa*, Rome 2019, pp. 35–44

CLEVELAND 1971
R.E. Spear, *Caravaggio and his Followers*, exh. cat., Cleveland Museum of Art, Cleveland, OH 1971

CORRADINI AND MARINI 1998
S. Corradini and M. Marini, 'The Earliest Account of Caravaggio in Rome', *The Burlington Magazine*, 140, no. 1138 (1998), pp. 25–8

CUSACK 1999
C.M. Cusack, 'Hagiography and History: The Legend of Saint Ursula', *Sydney Studies in Religion*, 2 (1999), pp. 89–104

DELL'ACQUA AND CINOTTI 1971
G.A. Dell'Acqua and M. Cinotti, *Il Caravaggio e le sue grandi opere da San Luigi dei Francesi*, Milan 1971

ENGGASS AND BROWN 1970
R. Enggass and J. Brown, *Italy and Spain, 1600–1750: Sources and Documents*, Englewood Cliffs, NJ 1970

GILBERT 1995
C. Gilbert, *Caravaggio and his Two Cardinals*, University Park, PA 1995

GRAHAM-DIXON 2010
A. Graham-Dixon, *Caravaggio: A Life Sacred and Profane*, London 2010

KEITH 1998
L. Keith, 'Three Paintings by Caravaggio', *National Gallery Technical Bulletin*, 19 (1998), pp. 37–51

LANGDON 2016
H. Langdon, *The Lives of Caravaggio*, London 2016, esp. G. Baglione, 'The Life of Michelangelo da Caravaggio, Painter' (1642), G.P. Bellori, 'Michelangelo da Caravaggio' (1672) and G. Mancini, 'On Michelangelo Merisi da Caravaggio' (1617–21)

LONDON 1982
C. Whitfield and J. Martineau, *Painting in Naples, 1606–1705: From Caravaggio to Giordano*, exh. cat., Royal Academy of Arts, London 1982

LONDON 2005
F. Bologna et al., *Caravaggio: The Final Years*, exh. cat., The National Gallery, London 2005

LONDON, DUBLIN AND EDINBURGH 2016–17
L. Treves et al., *Beyond Caravaggio*, exh. cat., The National Gallery, London; National Gallery of Ireland, Dublin; and Scottish National Gallery, Edinburgh; London, Dublin and Edinburgh 2016–17

MACIOCE 2023
S. Macioce, *Michelangelo Merisi da Caravaggio : documenti, fonti e inventari, 1513–1883*, 3rd edn, Rome 2023

MILAN 2017–18
R. Vodret et al., *Dentro Caravaggio*, exh. cat., Palazzo Reale, Milan 2017–18

MILAN AND PARIS 2014
F. Cappelletti and A. Lemoine (eds), *Les bas-fonds du baroque: la Rome du vice et de la misère*, exh. cat., Académie de France à Rome–Villa Médicis and Petit Palais–Musée des Beaux-Arts de la Ville de Paris, Milan [pub.] and Paris 2014

NAPLES 1963
G. Scavizzi (ed.), *Caravaggio e caravaggeschi*, exh. cat., Palazzo Reale, Naples 1963

NAPLES 2014–15
M.C. Terzaghi (ed.), *Tanzio da Varallo incontra Caravaggio: pittura a Napoli nel primo Seicento*, exh. cat., Gallerie d'Italia, Palazzo Zevallos Stigliano, Naples 2014–15

NAPLES 2019
M.C. Terzaghi (ed.), *Caravaggio a Napoli*, exh. cat., Museo e Real Bosco di Capodimonte, Naples 2019

PACELLI AND BOLOGNA 1980
V. Pacelli and F. Bologna, 'Caravaggio, 1610 : la "Sant'Orsola confitta dal Tiranno" per Marcantonio Doria', *Prospettiva*, 23 (1980), pp. 24–45

PARIS 2018–19
F. Cappelletti, M.C. Terzaghi and P. Curie (eds), *Caravage à Rome: amis et ennemis*, exh. cat., Musée Jacquemart-André, Paris 2018–19

ROME, MILAN AND VICENZA 2004
L'ultimo Caravaggio: il martirio di Sant'Orsola restaurato: Collezione Banca Intesa, exh. cat., Galleria Borghese, Rome; Pinacoteca Ambrosiana, Milan; and Gallerie di Palazzo Leoni Montanari, Vicenza; Rome, Milan and Vicenza 2004

SANDRART 1675
J. von Sandrart, *L'academia todesca della architectura, scultura e pittura, oder Teutsche Academie der edlen Bau-, Bild- und Mahlerey-Künste … durch Joachim von Sandrart auf Stockau*: www.google.co.uk/books/edition/L_academia_todesca_della_architectura_sc/RXZXDGs0nvAC?hl=en&gbpv=0 [accessed October 2023]

SANTAMARIA 2019
R. Santamaria, 'Marcantonio Doria collezionista e committente di Caravaggio tra Genova e Napoli', in A. Orlando et al., *Caravaggio e i genovesi: committenti, collezionisti, pittori*, exh. cat., Palazzo della Meridiana, Genoa 2019, pp. 118–29

SCIBERRAS 2023
K. Sciberras, *Art as Life: Caravaggio in Malta*, Valletta 2023

SPEAR 2020
R.E. Spear, *Caravaggio's Cardsharps on Trial: Thwaytes v. Sotheby's*, London 2020

SPEZZAFERRO 1971
L. Spezzaferro, *La cultura del cardinal Del Monte e il primo tempo del Caravaggio*, Florence 1971

SPINOSA 2010
N. Spinosa, *Pittura del Seicento a Napoli*, 2 vols, Naples 2010

VALLETTA (MALTA) 2007
C. de Giorgio and K. Sciberras (eds), *Caravaggio and Paintings of Realism in Malta*, exh. cat., St. John's Co-Cathedral, Valletta 2007

VODRET 2010
R. Vodret, *Caravaggio: The Complete Works*, Milan 2010

Photographic credits

BRUGES
© Stedelijke Musea Brugge: 34, 35.

COLOGNE
© Vassil Asjac: 37.

DUBLIN
Photo © The National Gallery of Ireland, Dublin: 20.

FLORENCE
Biblioteca Marucelliana, Florence © akg-images/Rabatti & Domingie: 4.

FORT WORTH, TEXAS
Kimbell Art Museum, Fort Worth, Texas © akg-images/Erich Lessing: 12.

IMOLA
Church of San Nicolò and San Domenico, Imola © photo Sergio Orselli, courtesy UCD/Diocesan Museum of Imola: 32.

LONDON
© The National Gallery, London: 7, 21, 30.

Royal Collection Trust/© His Majesty King Charles III 2024: 10.

MADRID
Museo Thyssen-Bornemisza, Madrid © Museo Thyssen-Bornemisza, Madrid/Scala, Florence: 17.

MILAN
Pinacoteca di Brera, Milan © akg-images/Mondadori Portfolio/Mauro Magliani: 26.

NAPLES
© Archivio di Stato, Napoli: 6.

Church of Pio Monte della Misericordia © Scala, Florence/Luciano Romano: 27.

Intesa Sanpaolo Collection Gallerie d'Italia – Napoli © Archivio Patrimonio Artistico Intesa Sanpaolo/foto Luciano Pedicini, Napoli: 1, 2, 3, 5.

NEW YORK
© The Metropolitan Museum of Art, New York: 13, 31, 36.

PARIS
Musée du Louvre, Paris: © RMN-Grand Palais/Mathieu Rabeau: 24, 29.

ROME
Galleria Borghese, Rome © Scala, Florence: 8, 9, 23, 25.

Galleria Doria Pamphilj, Rome © De Agostini Picture Library, Scala, Florence: 16.

Pinacoteca Capitolina, Rome © Scala, Florence: 11.

Sant'Agostino, Rome: © akg-images/MPortfolio/Electa: 22.

San Luigi dei Francesi, Rome: © akg-images/Mondadori Portfolio/Mauro Magliani: 18, 19.

San Luigi dei Francesi, Rome © Scala, Florence/LucianoRomano: 15.

ST PETERSBURG
The State Hermitage Museum, St Petersburg © Scala, Florence: 14.

VALLETTA
St John's Co-Cathedral, Valletta, Malta © Scala, Florence: 28.

VENICE
Gallerie dell'Accademia, Venice © Luisa Ricciarini/Bridgeman Images: 33.

List of lenders and exhibited works

INTESA SANPAOLO COLLECTION
GALLERIE D'ITALIA – NAPOLI
Michelangelo Merisi da Caravaggio (1571–1610)
The Martyrdom of Saint Ursula, 1610
Oil on canvas, 143 × 180 cm

ARCHIVIO DI STATO
DI NAPOLI
Letter from Lanfranco Massa to Marcantonio Doria, 11 May 1610
Ink on paper, 31 × 21.5 cm
Archivio di Doria d'Angri, parte II, b. 290, cc. 9–10

Acknowledgements

It is an immense pleasure and privilege to exhibit *The Martyrdom of Saint Ursula* in London for the first time in a generation, and I am indebted to the Banca Intesa Sanpaolo and Gallerie d'Italia for making this exhibition possible. I extend heartfelt thanks to all the team there, especially Michele Coppola, Executive Director of Art, Culture and Historical Heritage and Director of the Gallerie d'Italia, for sharing this masterpiece with us, and likewise to our colleagues at the Archivio di Stato di Napoli, for allowing us to reunite Massa's letter with the painting. I must single out Antonio Ernesto Denunzio, Head of Cultural Initiatives and Exhibitions and Deputy Director of the Gallerie d'Italia – Napoli, the most gracious and generous colleague one could wish for, who has supported this extraordinary loan every step of the way and has so readily shared his deep knowledge of the picture.

The scholarship on Caravaggio is too vast to thank individual authors for their contributions to our understanding of this endlessly fascinating artist, but I am particularly grateful to Helen Langdon and Letizia Treves, and to Gabriele Finaldi and Keith Christiansen, who read early drafts of this catalogue. Many National Gallery colleagues have cheered on this project and made the exhibition possible: my especial thanks to Siobhán Jolley, Larry Keith, Daniel Ralston, Jane Knowles, Sunnifa Hope, Giulia Segreto, Alessandra Isolan, Louise Nyborg, Lawrence Chiles, Karen Eslea and Margherita di Ceglie. In Publishing, Laura Lappin, Catherine Hooper, Suzanne Bosman and Jane Hyne have gone above and beyond to produce this catalogue in a very tight timeframe, for which I am extremely thankful.

Finally, I thank my husband Alex for his boundless encouragement.

Plates

HELEN BUTTON	SPAULDING, CAROL	STP7CL
HOUSE OF MIRTH	WHARTON, EDITH	STP7CL
HUMAN STAIN	ROTH, PHILIP	STP7CL
KAFKA A VERY SHORT INTRODUCTION	ROBERTSON, RITCHIE	STP7CL
LUCKY JIM	AMIS, KINGSLEY	STP7CL
MALIBU RISING	REID, TAYLOR JENKINS	STP7CL
MAN'S SEARCH FOR MEANING	FRANKL, VIKTOR	STP7CL
MODERN POETRY	SEUSS, DIANE	STP7CL
OUR DECLARATION	ALLEN, DANIELLE	STP7CL
PARIS FRANCE	STEIN, GERTRUDE	STP7CL
RYE BREAD MARRIAGE	WEISSMAN, MICHAELE	STP7CL
SAFEKEEPING	THOMAS, ABIGAIL	STP7CL
SELECTED STORIES	KAFKA, FRANZ	STP7CL
SILENCE	NHAT HANH, THICH	STP7CL
STORY GENIUS	CRON, LISA	STP7CL
SUMMER	WHARTON, EDITH	STP7CL
TESS OF THE DURBERVILLES	HARDY, THOMAS	STP7CL
TRUE GRIT	PORTIS, CHARLES	STP7CL
WHO SAYS	ZEIDNER, LISA	STP7CL
WOMAN IN WHITE	COLLINS, WILKIE	STP7CL
DAISY JONES AND THE SIX	REID, TAYLOR JENKINS	STP7CL D
ANCILLARY JUSTICE	LECKIE, ANN	STP7CL G
ON THE CALCULATION OF VOLUME BOOK I	BALLE, SOLVEJ	TPF STP2
ORBITAL	HARVEY, SAMANTHA	TPF STP2
SAFEKEEP	VAN DER WOUDEN, YAEL	TPF STP2
HEADSHOT		

CONTEMPT

Alberto Moravia

9781590171226

nyrb.com

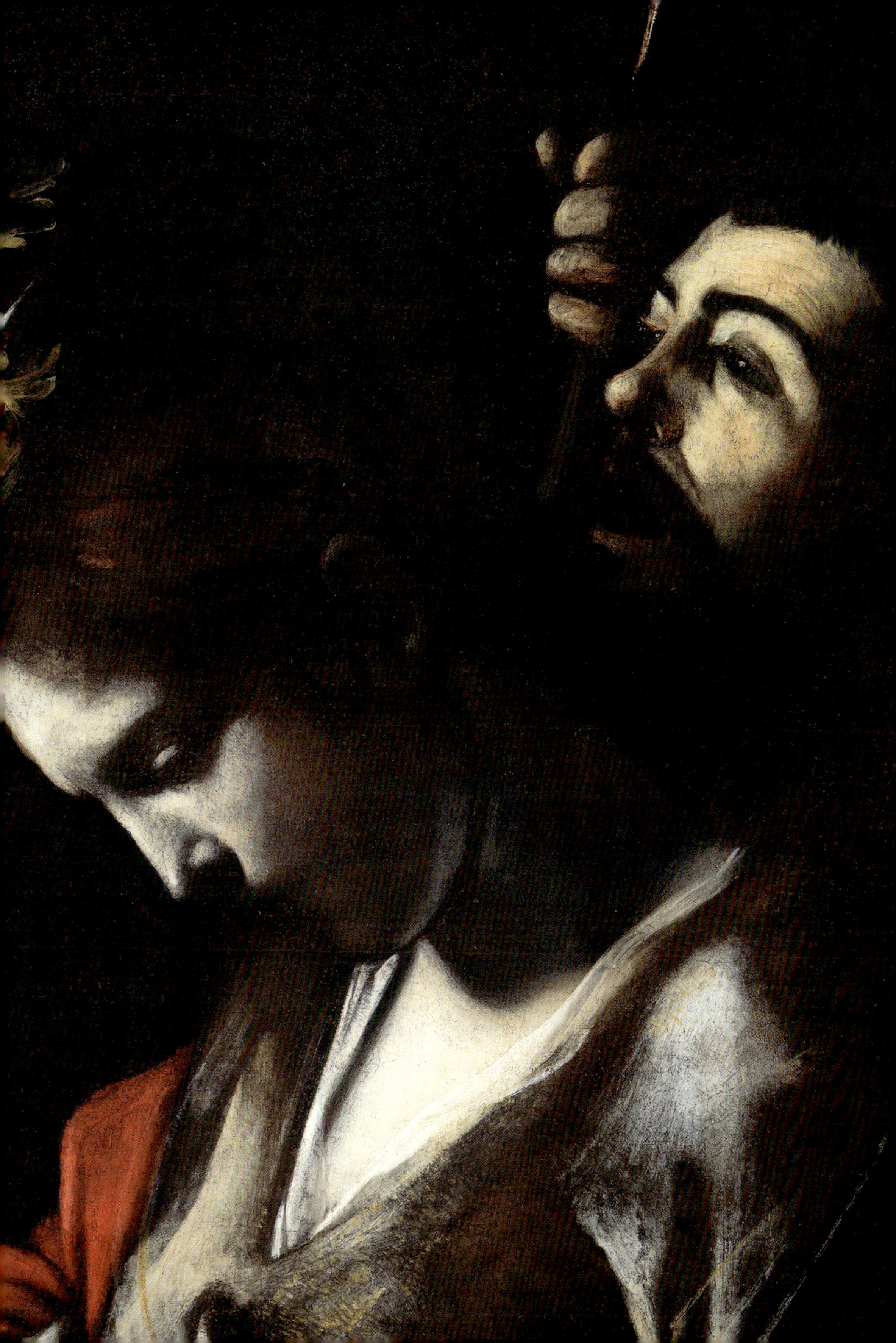

FIG. 1
The Martyrdom of Saint Ursula, 1610
Oil on canvas, 143 × 180 cm
Intesa Sanpaolo Collection
Gallerie d'Italia – Napoli

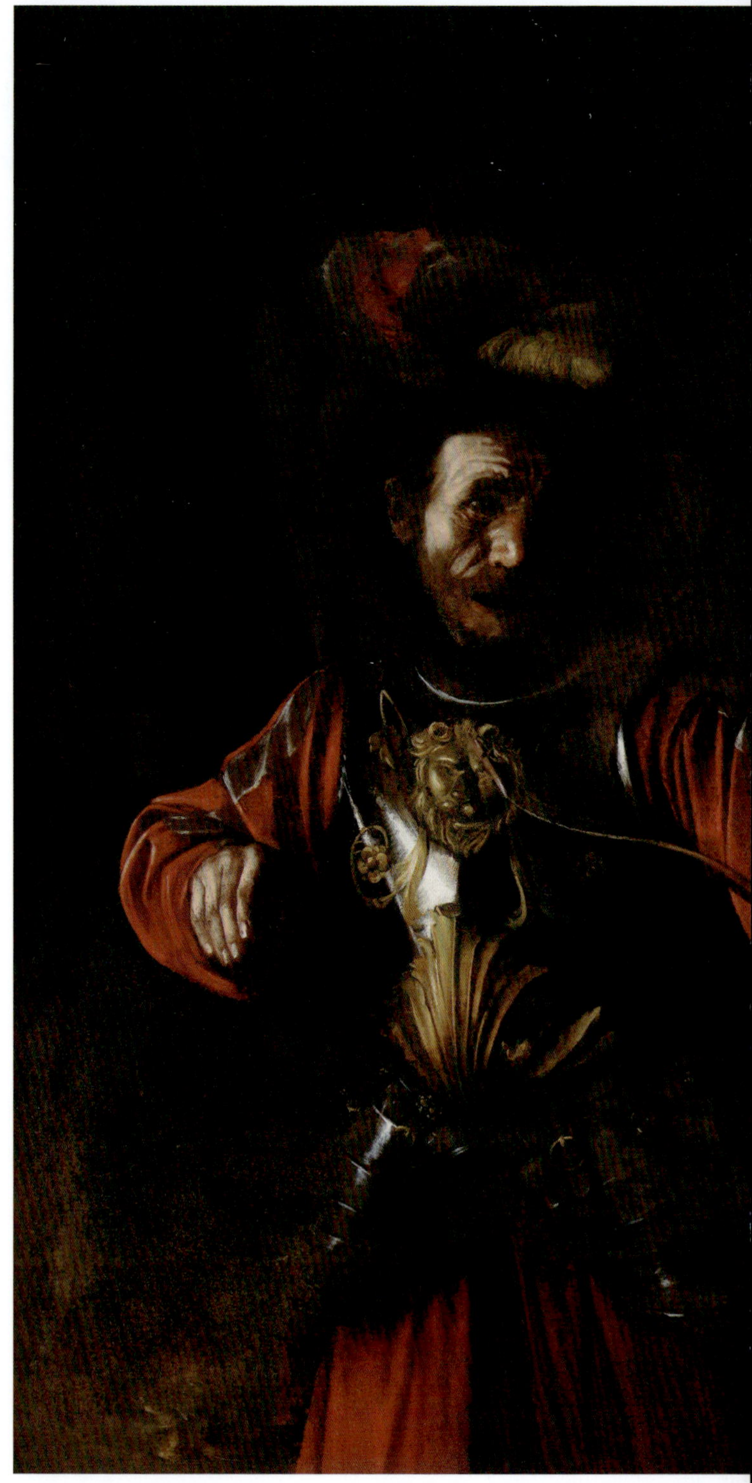

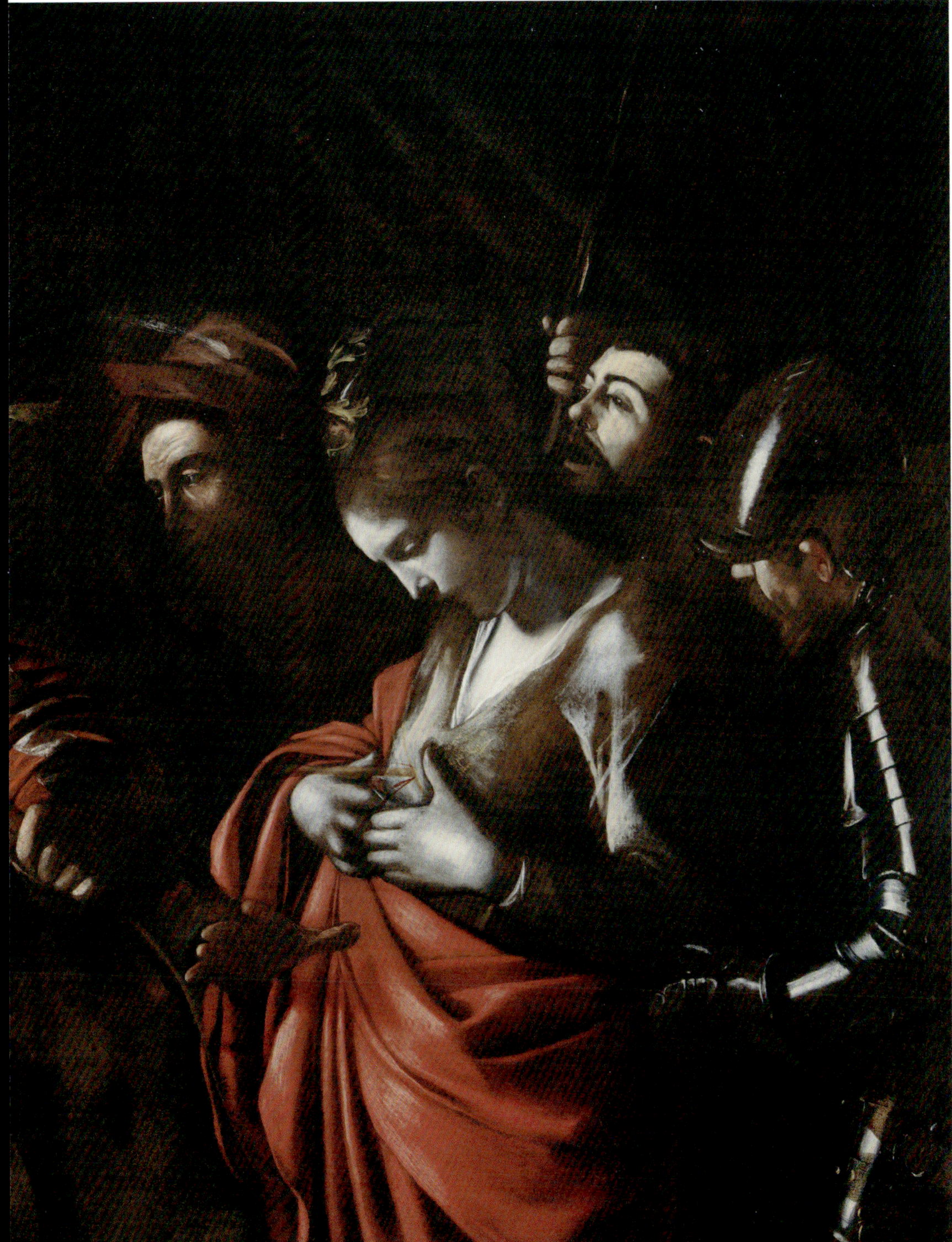

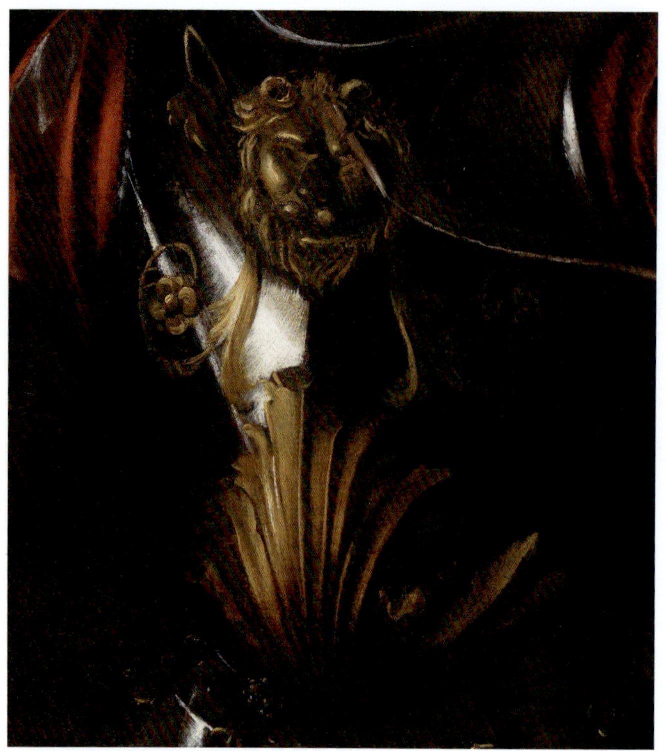

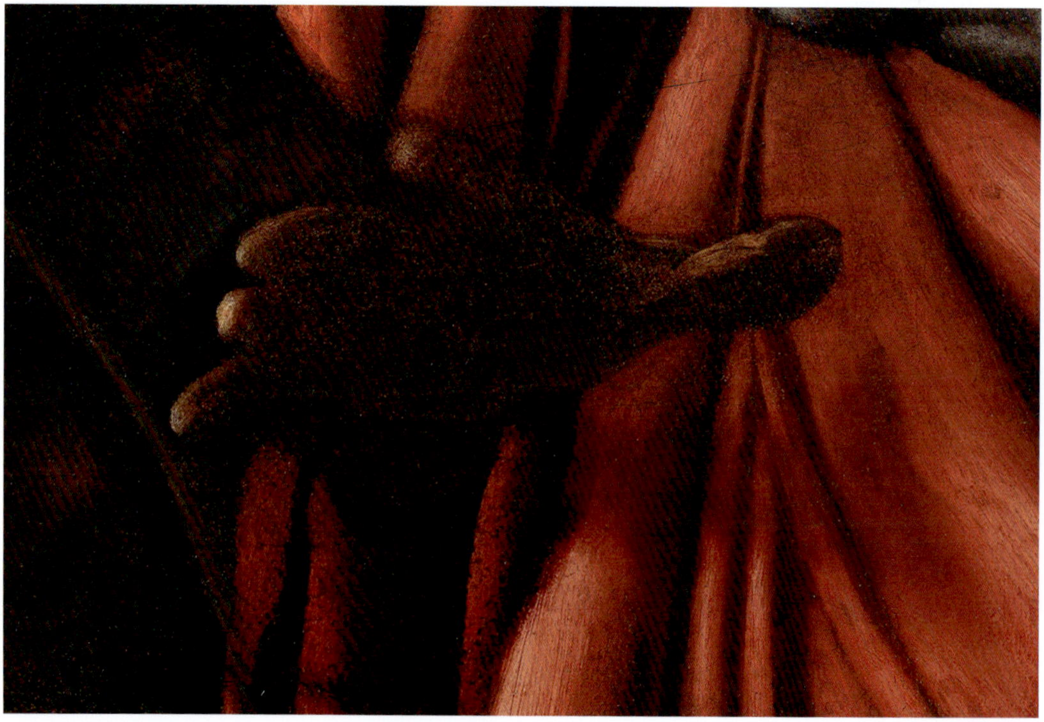

FIGS 2 and 3
Details from *The Martyrdom of Saint Ursula*, 1610

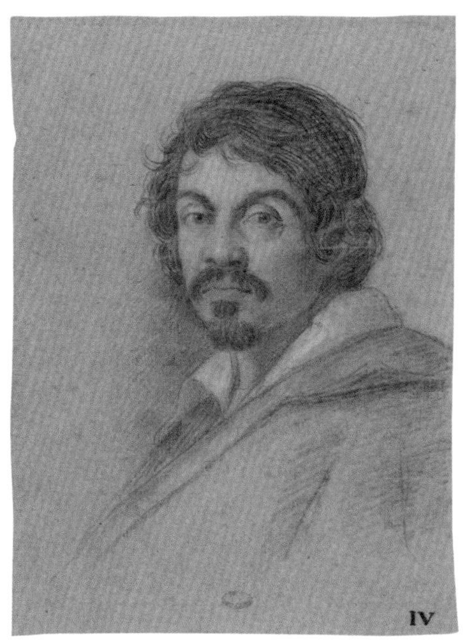

FIG. 4
Ottavio Leoni (1578–1630)
Portrait of Caravaggio, about 1621
Chalk on paper, 23.4 × 16.3 cm
Biblioteca Marucelliana, Florence

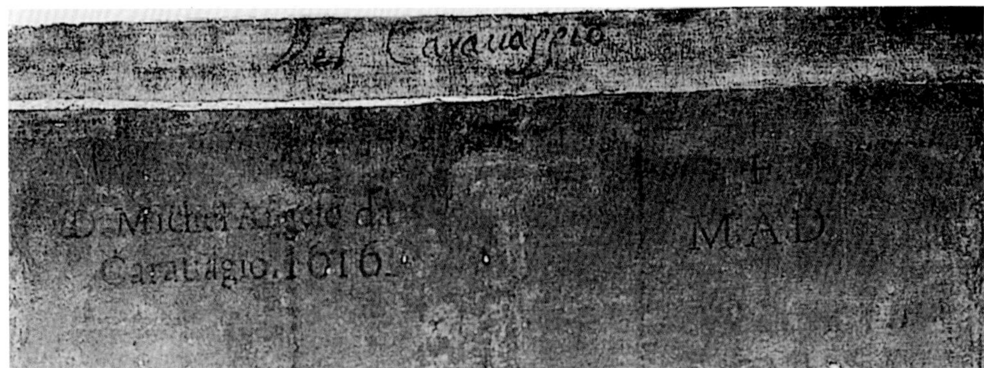

FIG. 5
Seventeenth-century inscriptions on the back of the canvas of *The Martyrdom of Saint Ursula*

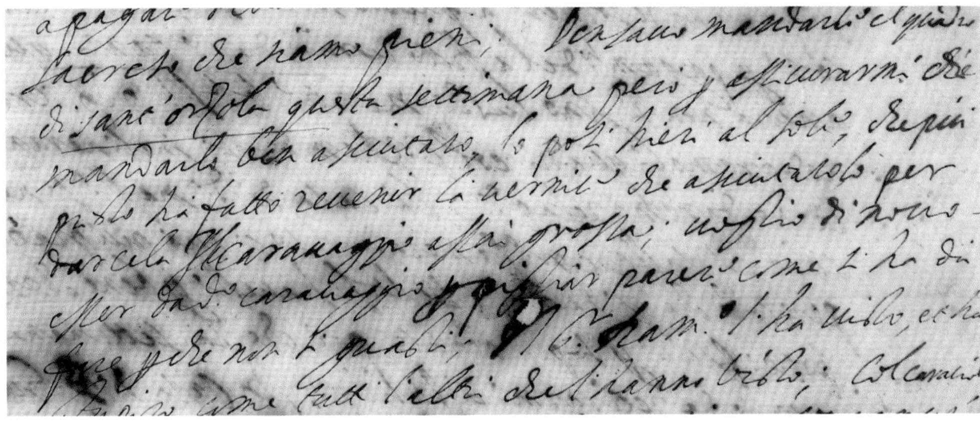

FIG. 6
Letter from Lanfranco Massa to Marcantonio Doria, 11 May 1610
Ink on paper, 31 × 21.5 cm
Archivio di Stato di Napoli

FIG. 7
Boy bitten by a Lizard,
about 1594–5
Oil on canvas, 66 × 49.5 cm
The National Gallery, London

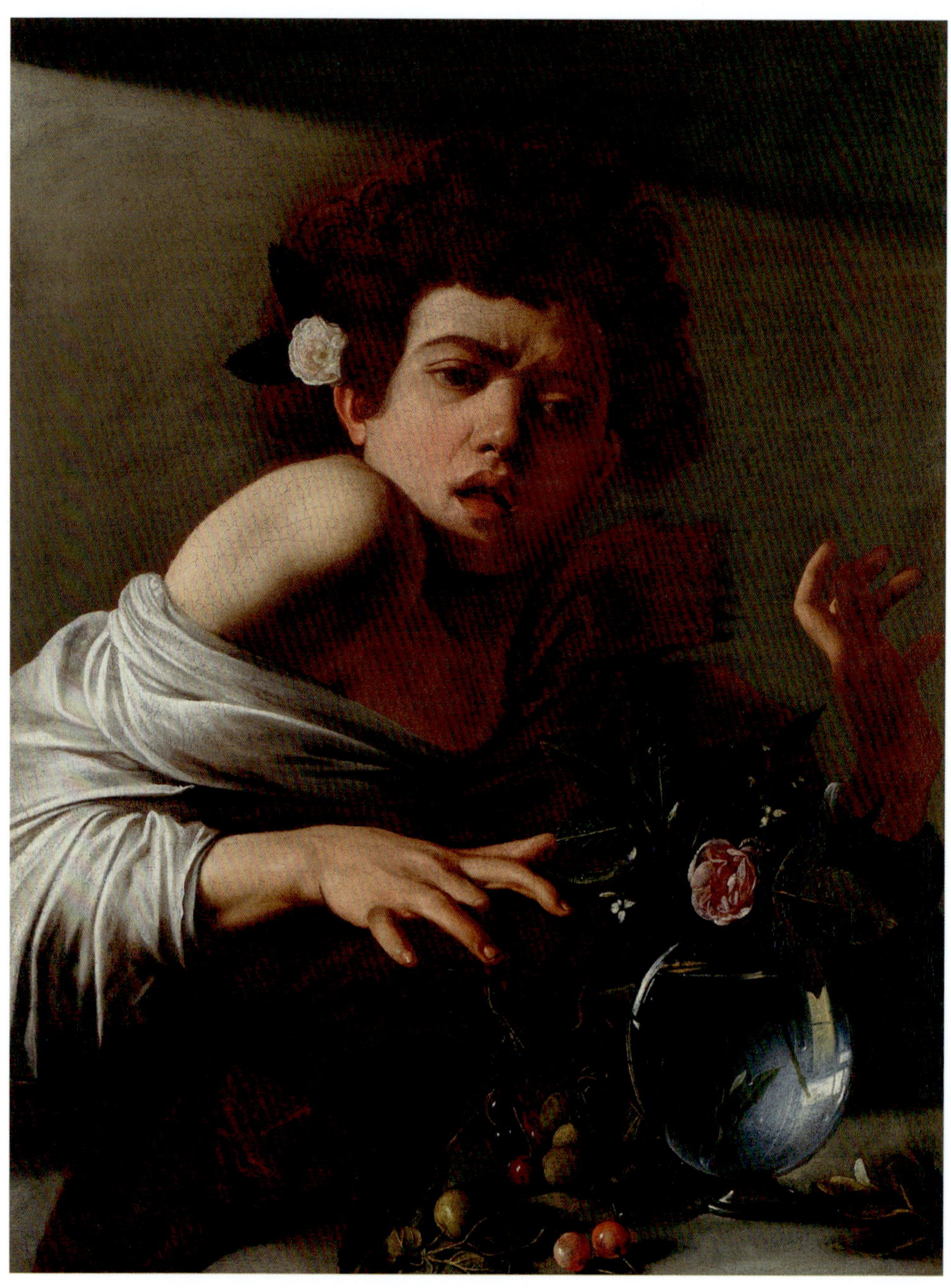

FIG. 8
Boy with a Basket of Fruit, 1594
Oil on canvas, 70 × 67 cm
Galleria Borghese, Rome

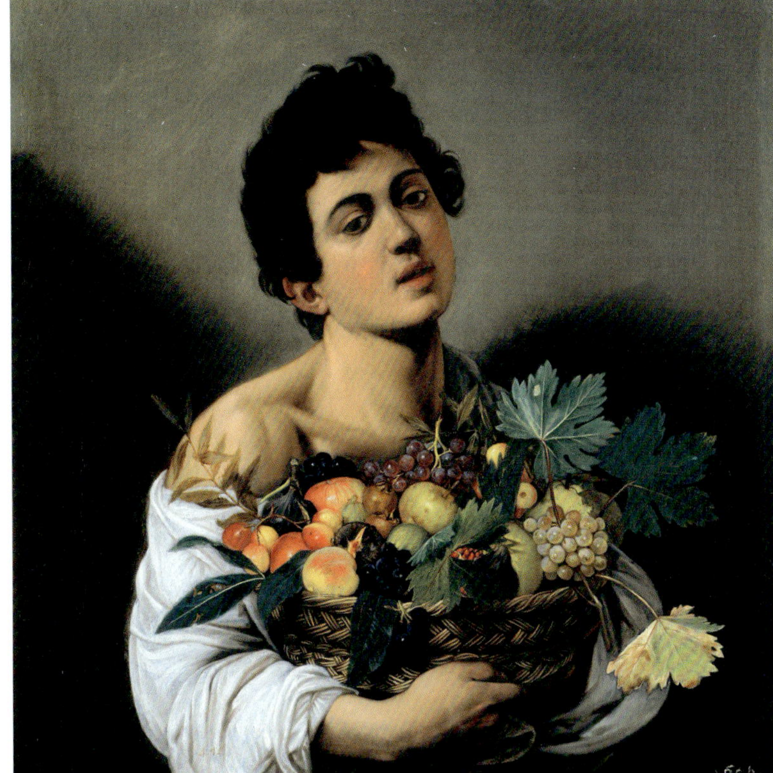

FIG. 9
Sick Bacchus, 1593
Oil on canvas, 66 × 52 cm
Galleria Borghese, Rome

FIG. 10
Boy peeling Fruit, about 1592–3
Oil on canvas, 63 × 53 cm
The Royal Collection / HM King Charles III

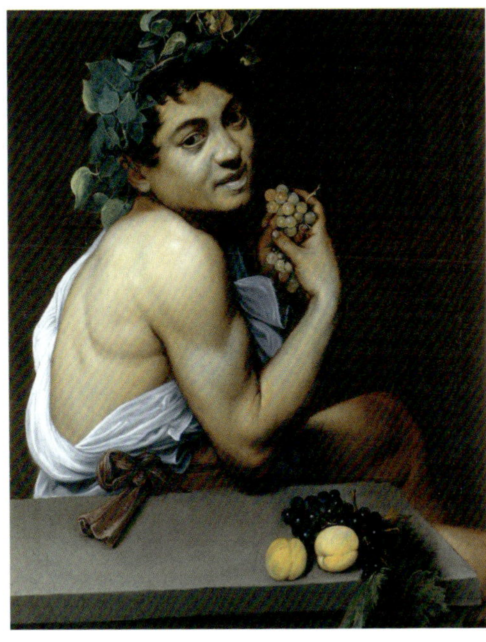

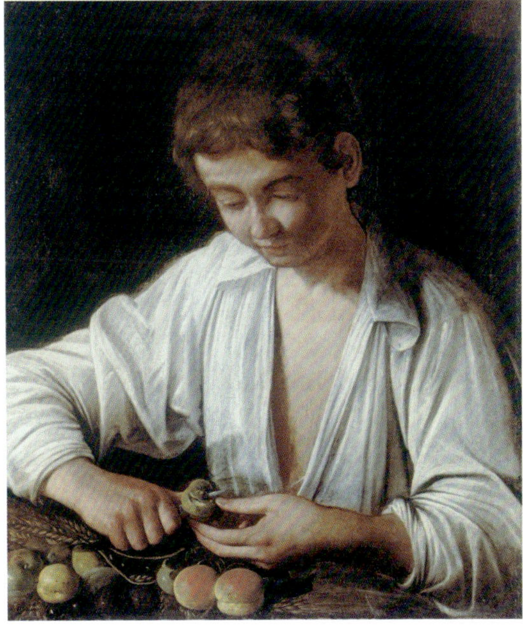

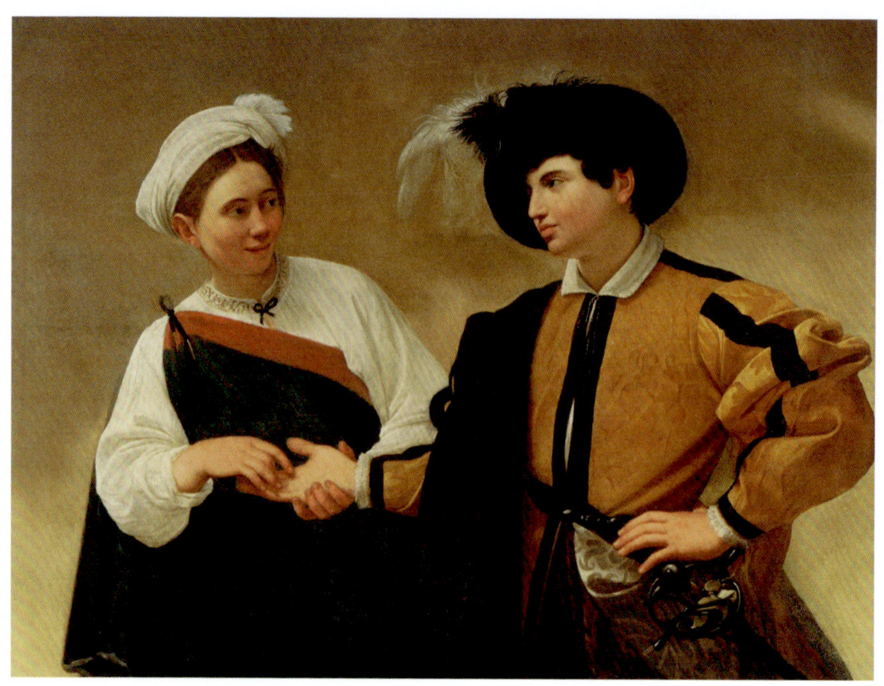

FIG. 11
The Fortune Teller, about 1594
Oil on canvas, 115 × 150 cm
Pinacoteca Capitolina, Rome

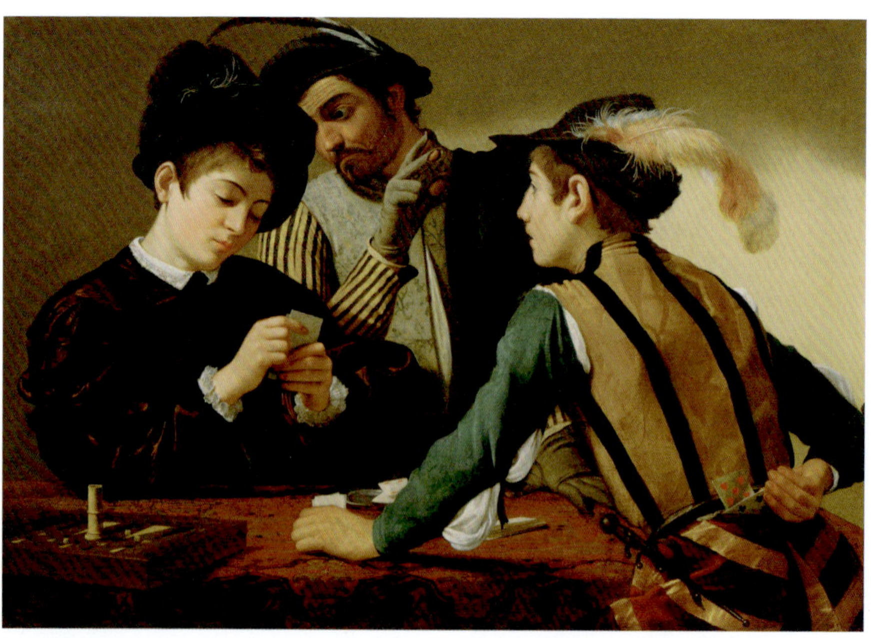

FIG. 12
The Cardsharps, about 1595
Oil on canvas, 94.2 × 130.9 cm
Kimbell Art Museum, Fort Worth, Texas

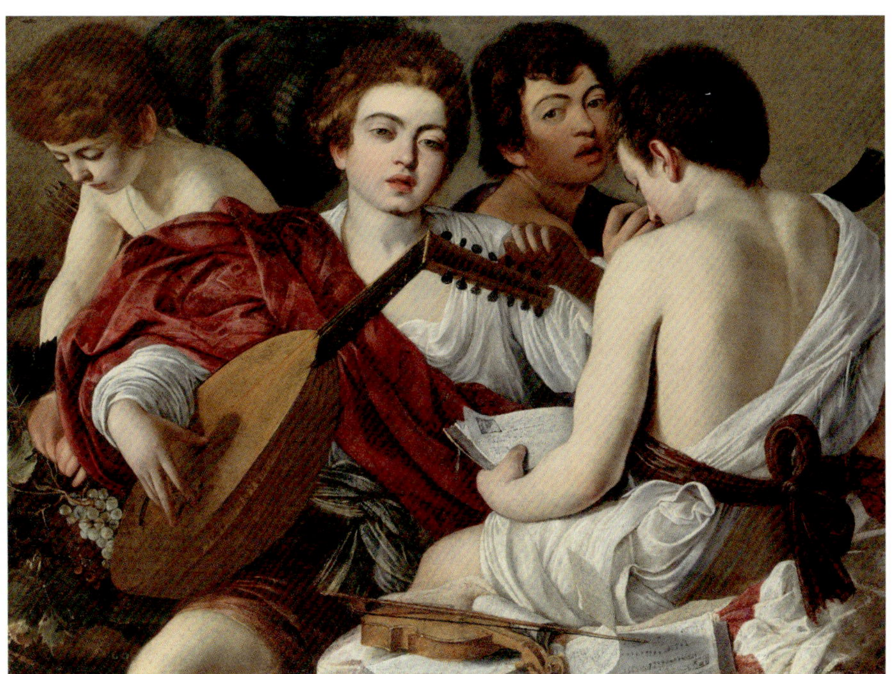

FIG. 13
The Musicians, 1597
Oil on canvas, 92.1 × 118.4 cm
The Metropolitan Museum of Art, New York, Rogers Fund, 1952

FIG. 14
The Lute Player, about 1600
Oil on canvas, 94 × 119 cm
The State Hermitage Museum, St Petersburg

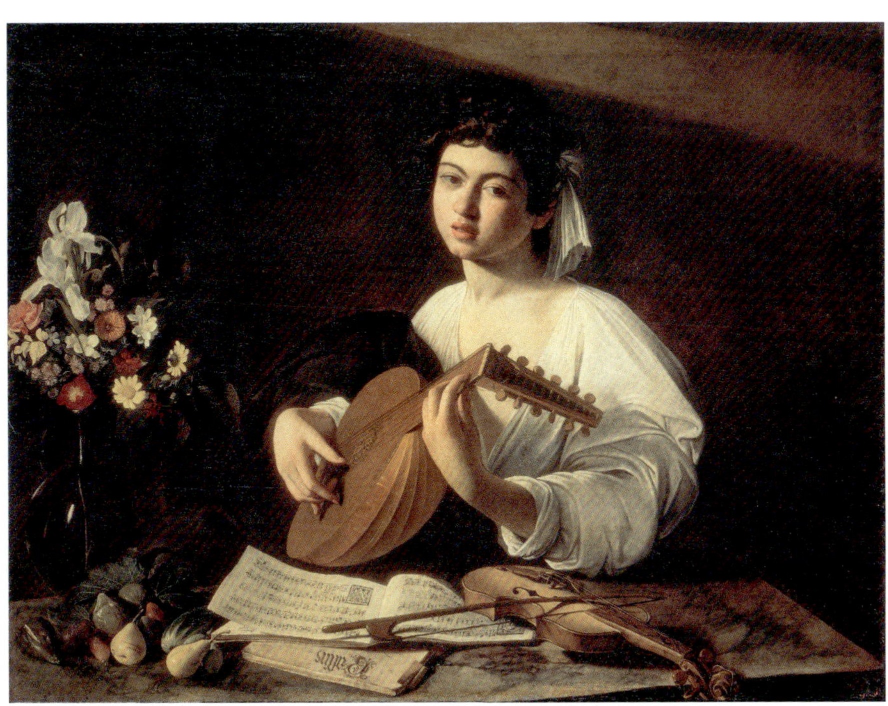

FIG. 15
The Contarelli Chapel, Church of San Luigi dei Francesi, Rome

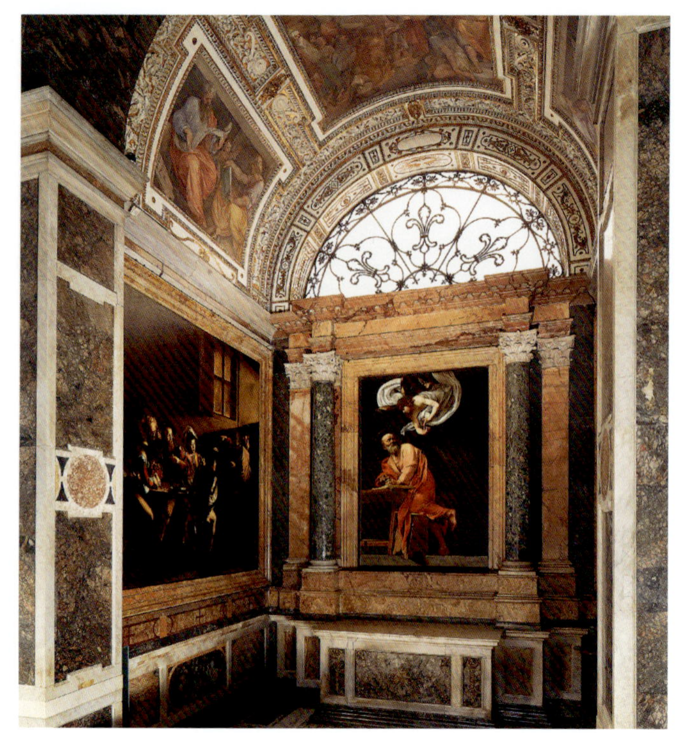

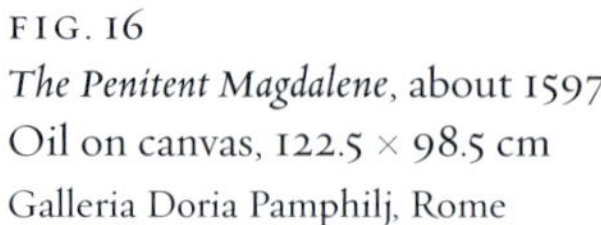

FIG. 16
The Penitent Magdalene, about 1597
Oil on canvas, 122.5 × 98.5 cm
Galleria Doria Pamphilj, Rome

FIG. 17
Saint Catherine of Alexandria, about 1598–9
Oil on canvas, 173 × 133 cm
Museo Nacional Thyssen-Bornemisza, Madrid

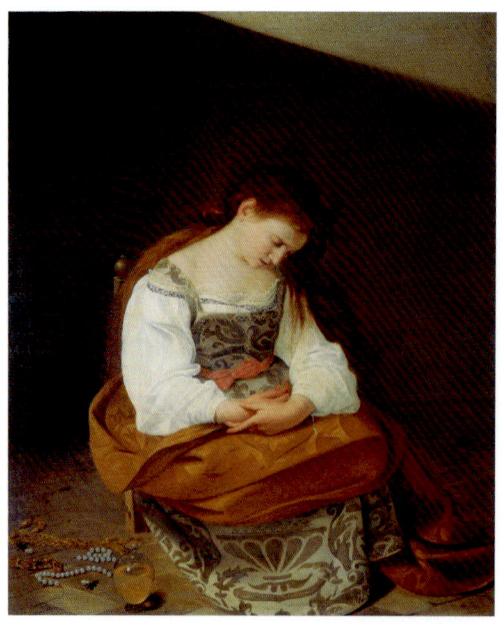

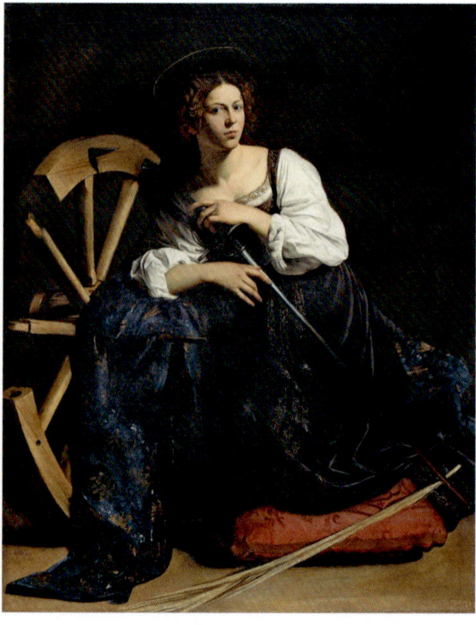

FIG. 18
The Calling of Saint Matthew, 1599–1600
Oil on canvas, 328 × 348 cm
Church of San Luigi dei Francesi, Rome

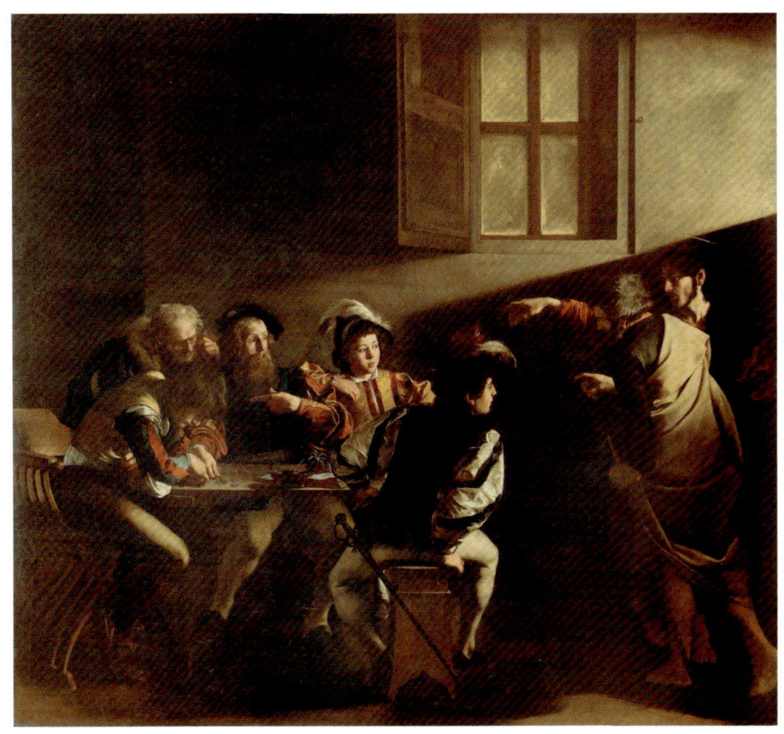

FIG. 19
The Martyrdom of Saint Matthew, 1599–1600
Oil on canvas, 323 × 343 cm
Church of San Luigi dei Francesi, Rome

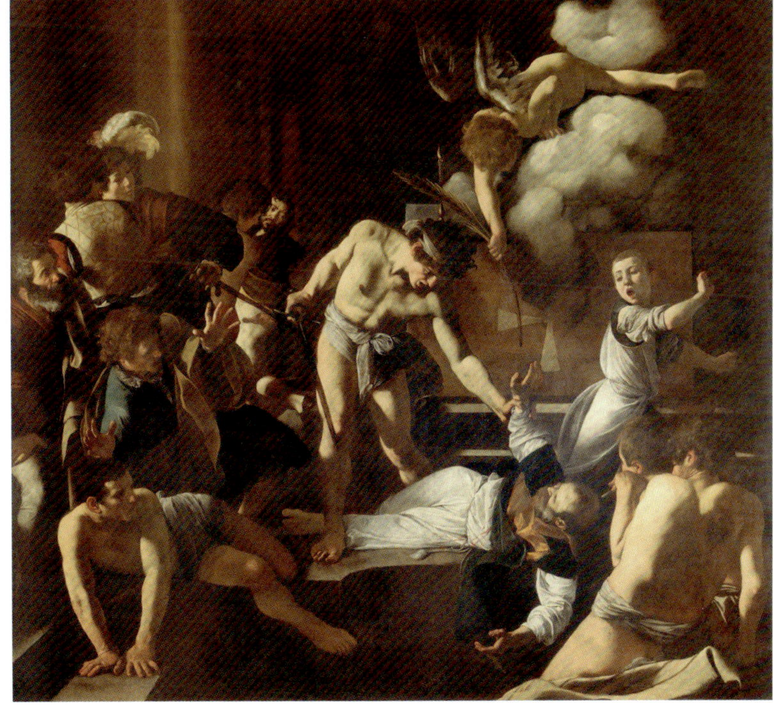

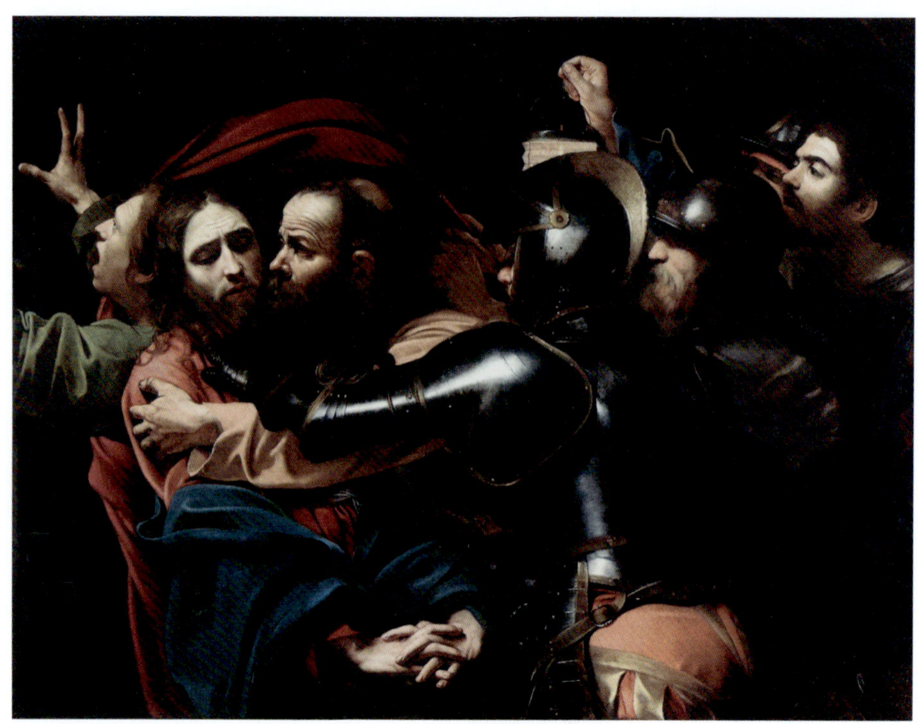

FIG. 20
The Taking of Christ, 1602
Oil on canvas, 133.5 × 169.5 cm
On indefinite loan to the National Gallery of Ireland from the Jesuit Community, Leeson St, Dublin who acknowledge the kind generosity of the late Dr Marie Lea-Wilson, 1992

FIG. 21
The Supper at Emmaus, 1601
Oil on canvas, 141 × 196.2 cm
The National Gallery, London

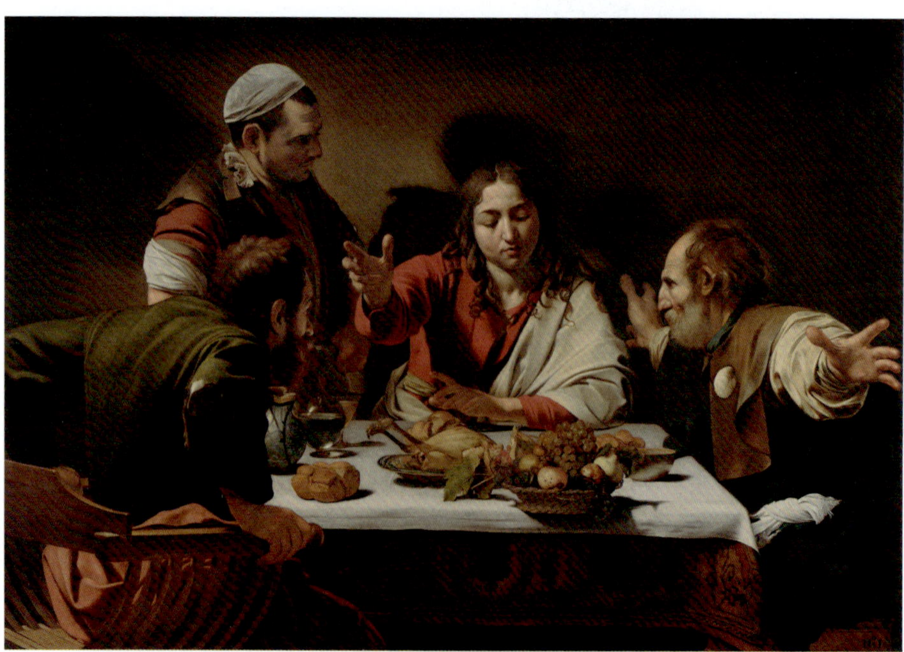

FIG. 22
The Madonna of Loreto, 1604–6
Oil on canvas, 260 × 150 cm
Church of Sant'Agostino, Rome

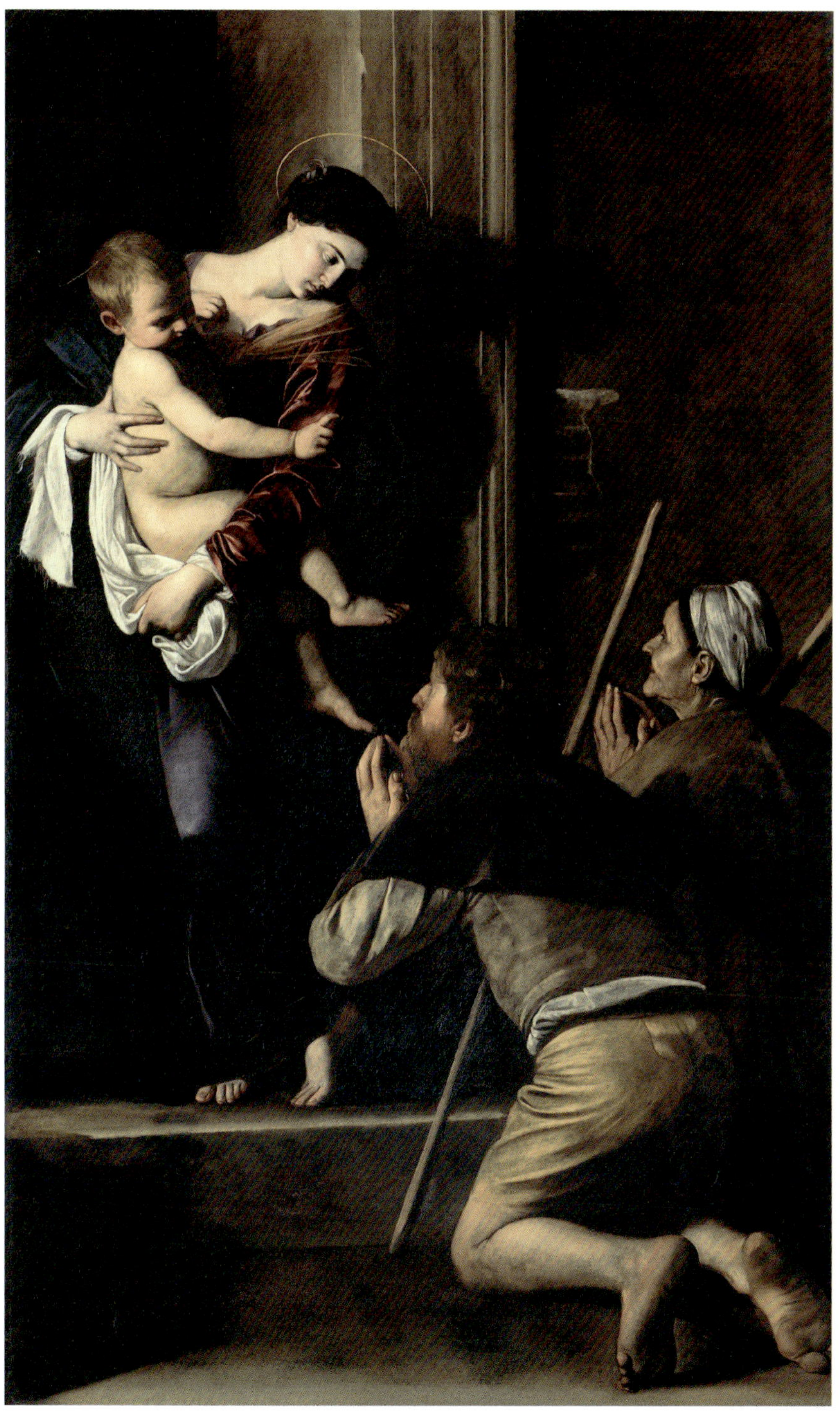

FIG. 23
Madonna and Child with Saint Anne, 1605–6
Oil on canvas, 292 × 211 cm
Galleria Borghese, Rome

FIG. 24
The Death of the Virgin, 1606
Oil on canvas, 369 × 245 cm
Musée du Louvre, Paris

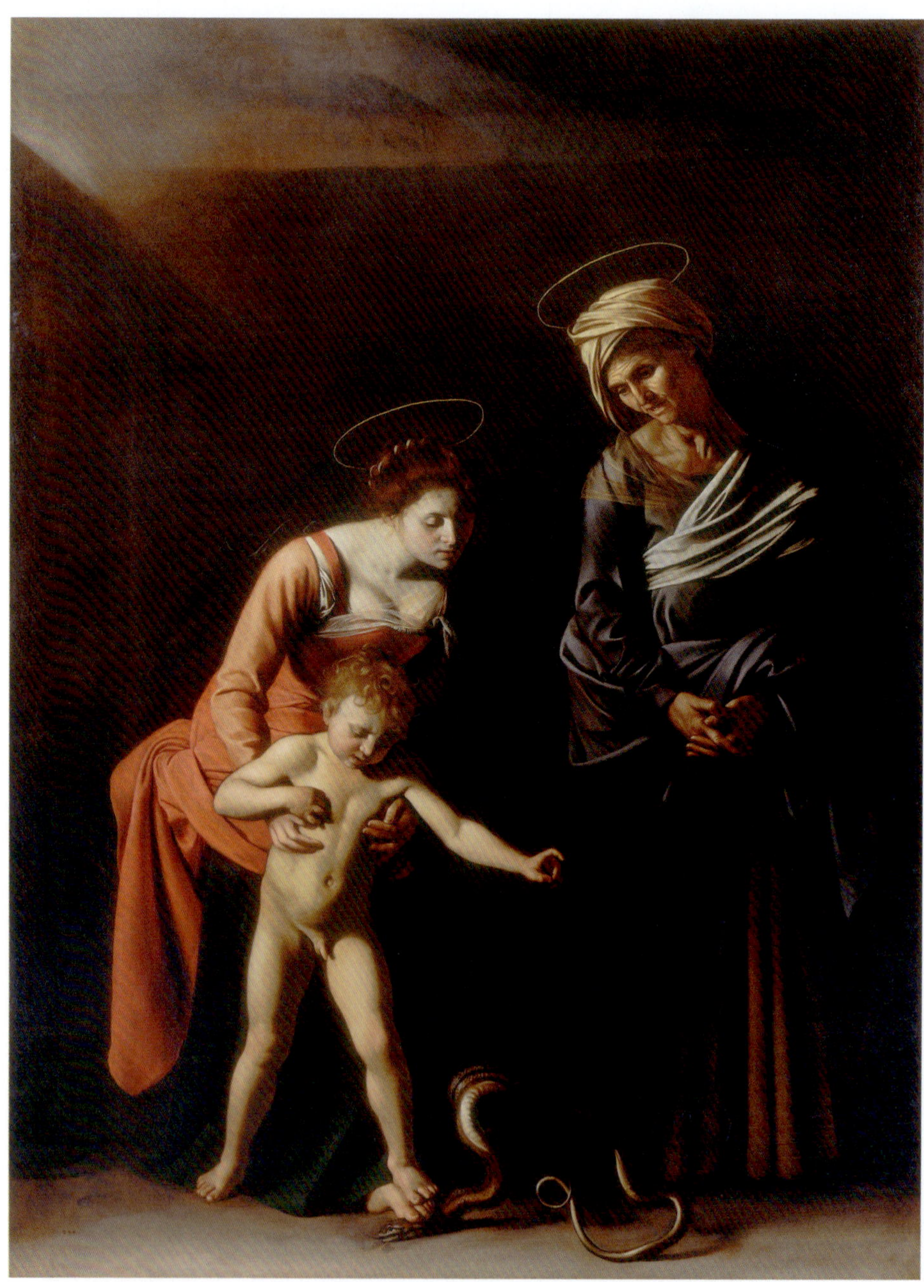

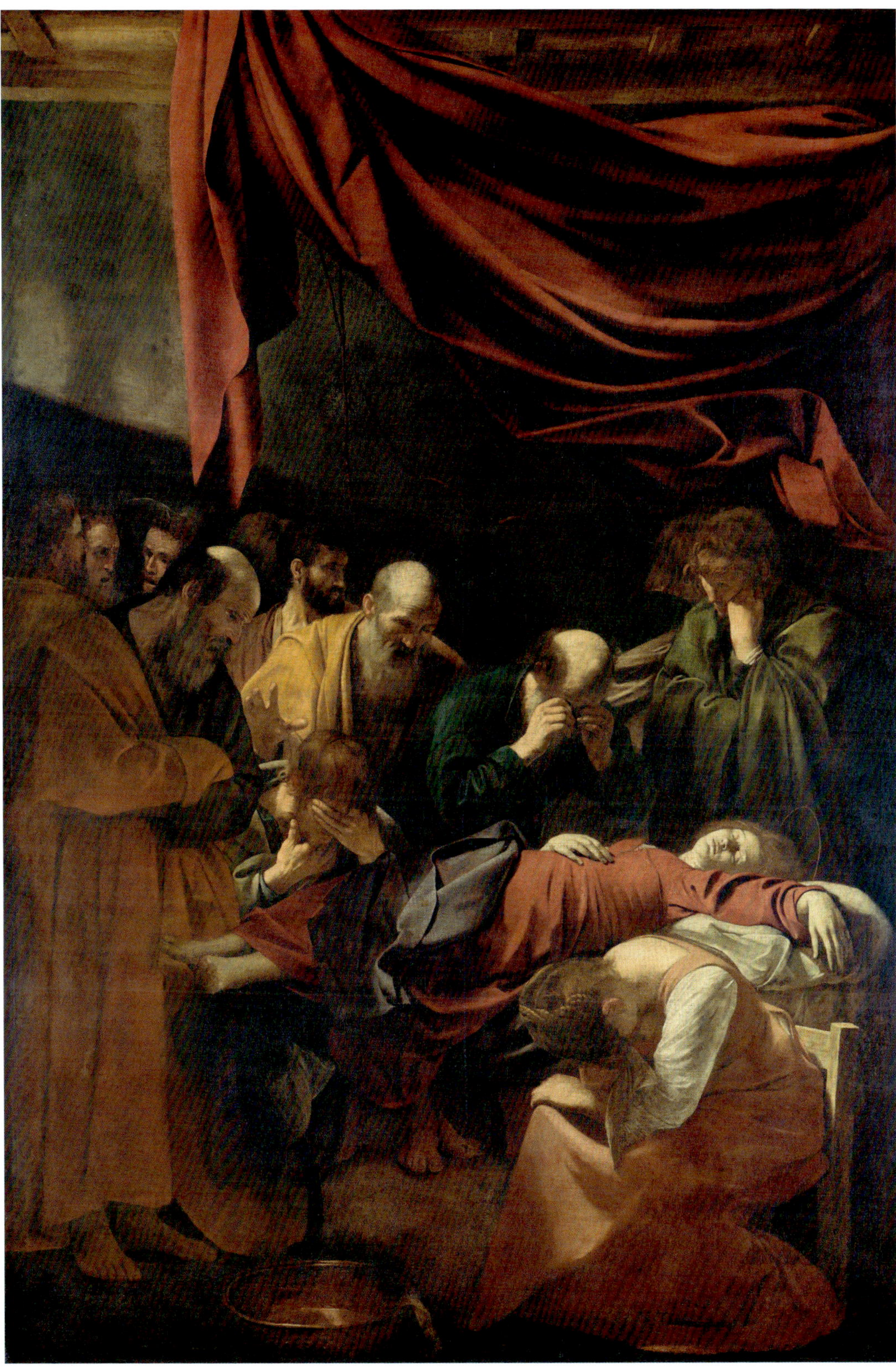

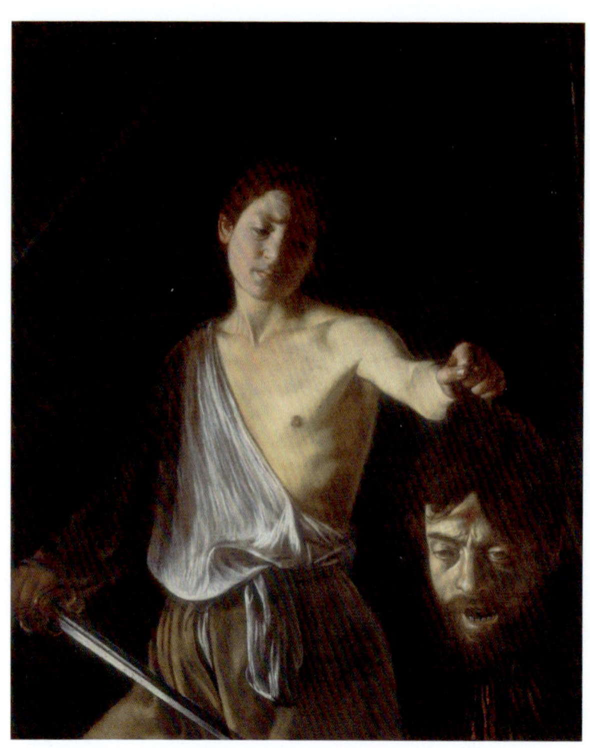

FIG. 25
David with the Head of Goliath, about 1610
Oil on canvas, 125 × 100 cm
Galleria Borghese, Rome

FIG. 26
The Supper at Emmaus, 1606
Oil on canvas, 141 × 175 cm
Pinacoteca di Brera, Milan

FIG. 27
The Seven Acts of Mercy, 1607
Oil on canvas, 390 × 260 cm
Church of Pio Monte della Misericordia, Naples

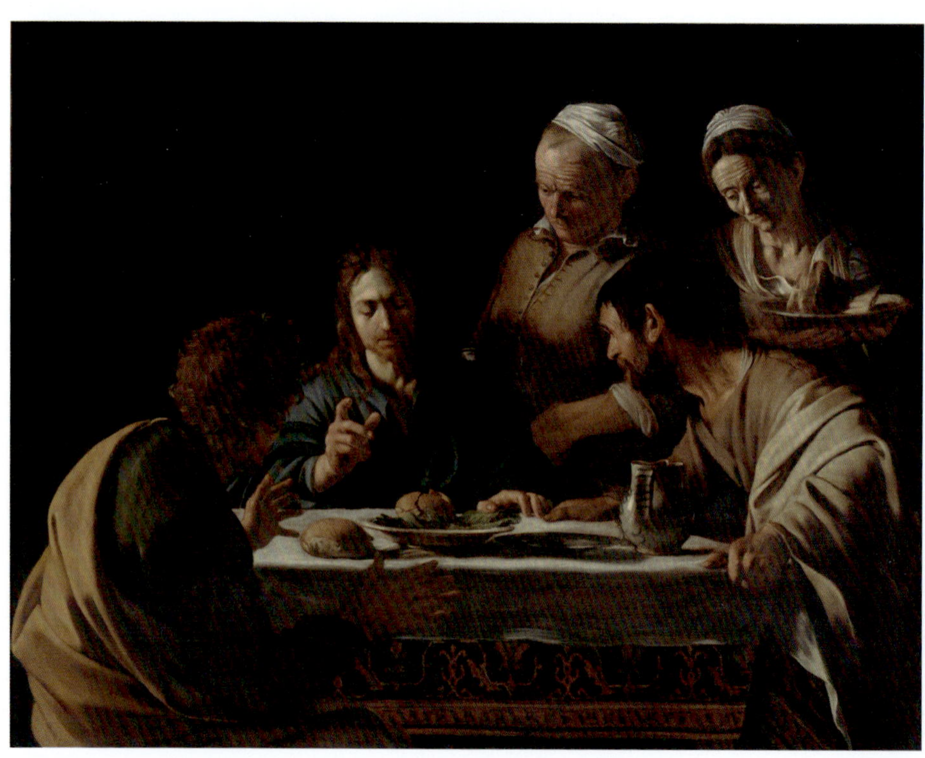

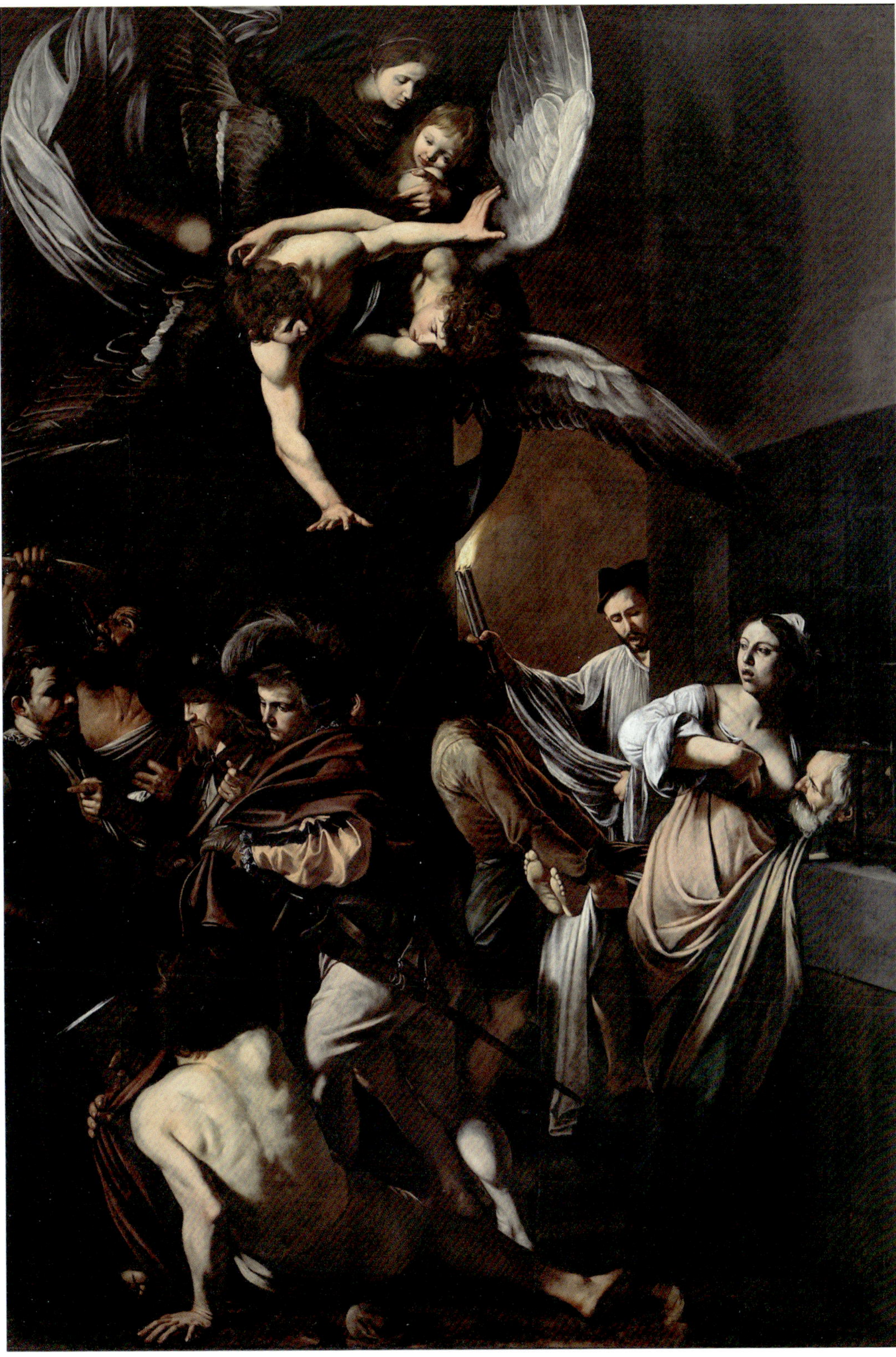

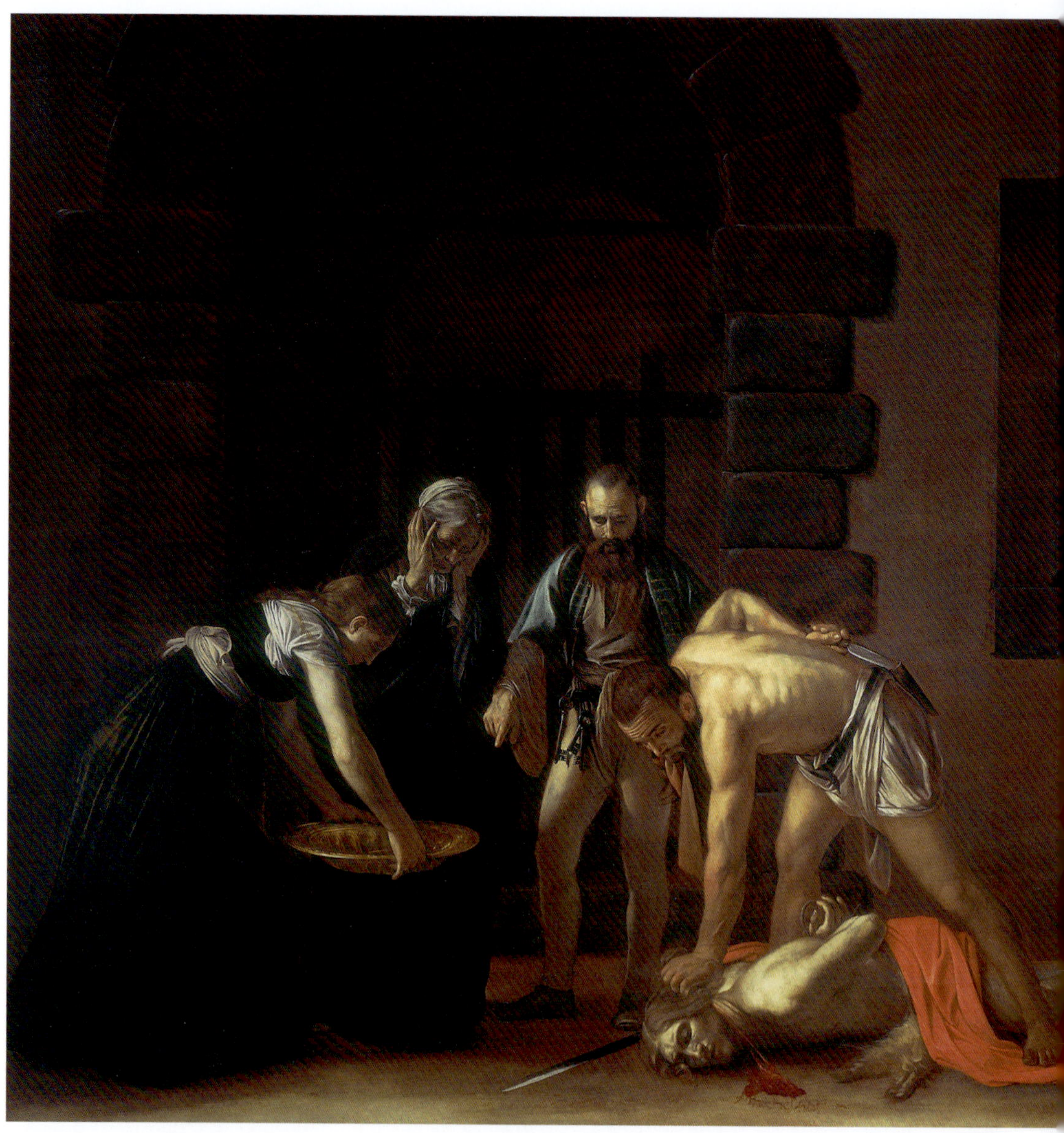

FIG. 28
The Beheading of John the Baptist, 1608
Oil on canvas, 360 × 520 cm
St John's Co-Cathedral, Valletta, Malta

FIG. 29
Alof de Wignacourt (1547–1622), Grand Master of the Order of Malta from 1601 to 1622, and his Page, 1607–8
Oil on canvas, 194 × 134 cm
Musée du Louvre, Paris

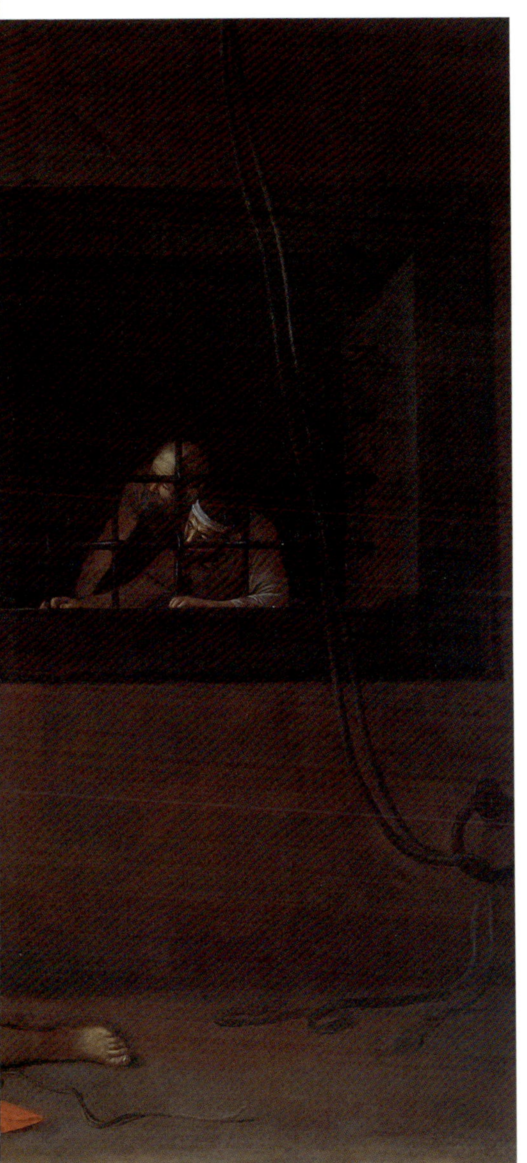

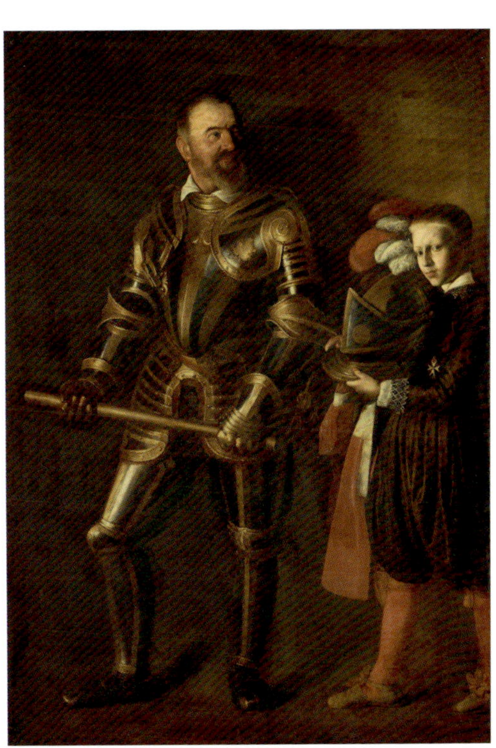

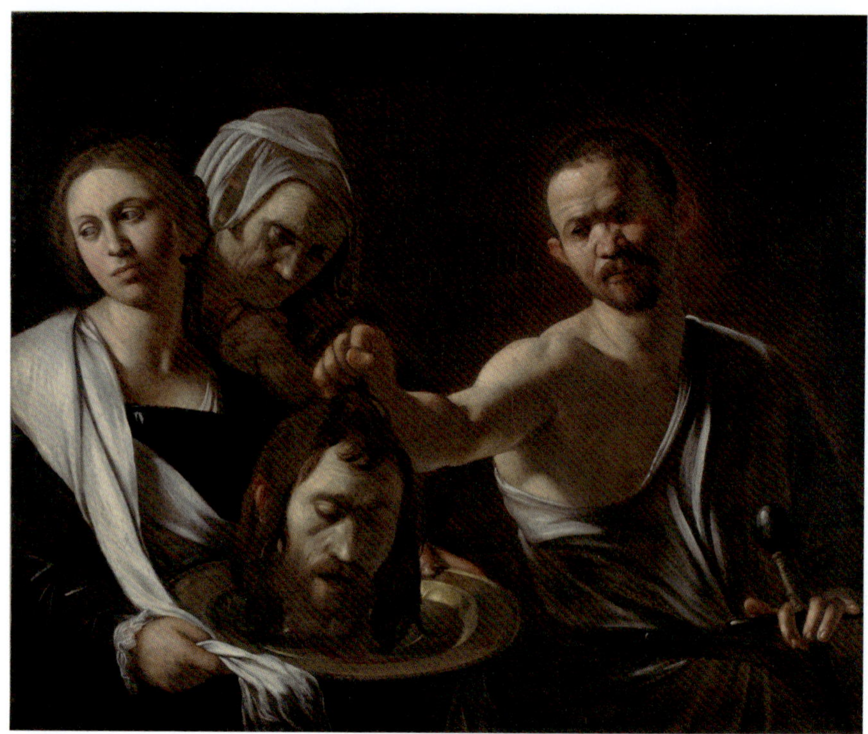

FIG. 30
Salome receives the Head of John the Baptist, about 1609–10
Oil on canvas, 91.5 × 106.7 cm
The National Gallery, London

FIG. 31
The Denial of Saint Peter, 1610
Oil on canvas, 94 × 125.4 cm
The Metropolitan Museum of Art, New York, Gift of Herman and Lila Shickman, and Purchase, Lila Acheson Wallace Gift, 1997

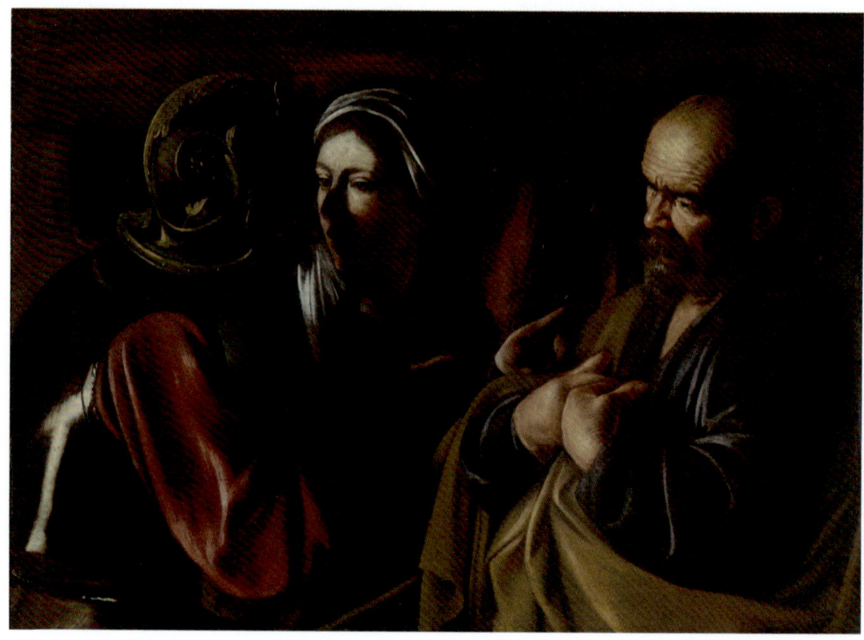

FIG. 32
Ludovico Carracci (1555–1619)
The Martyrdom of Saint Ursula, 1600
Oil on canvas, 343 × 229 cm
Church of San Nicolò e San Domenico, Imola

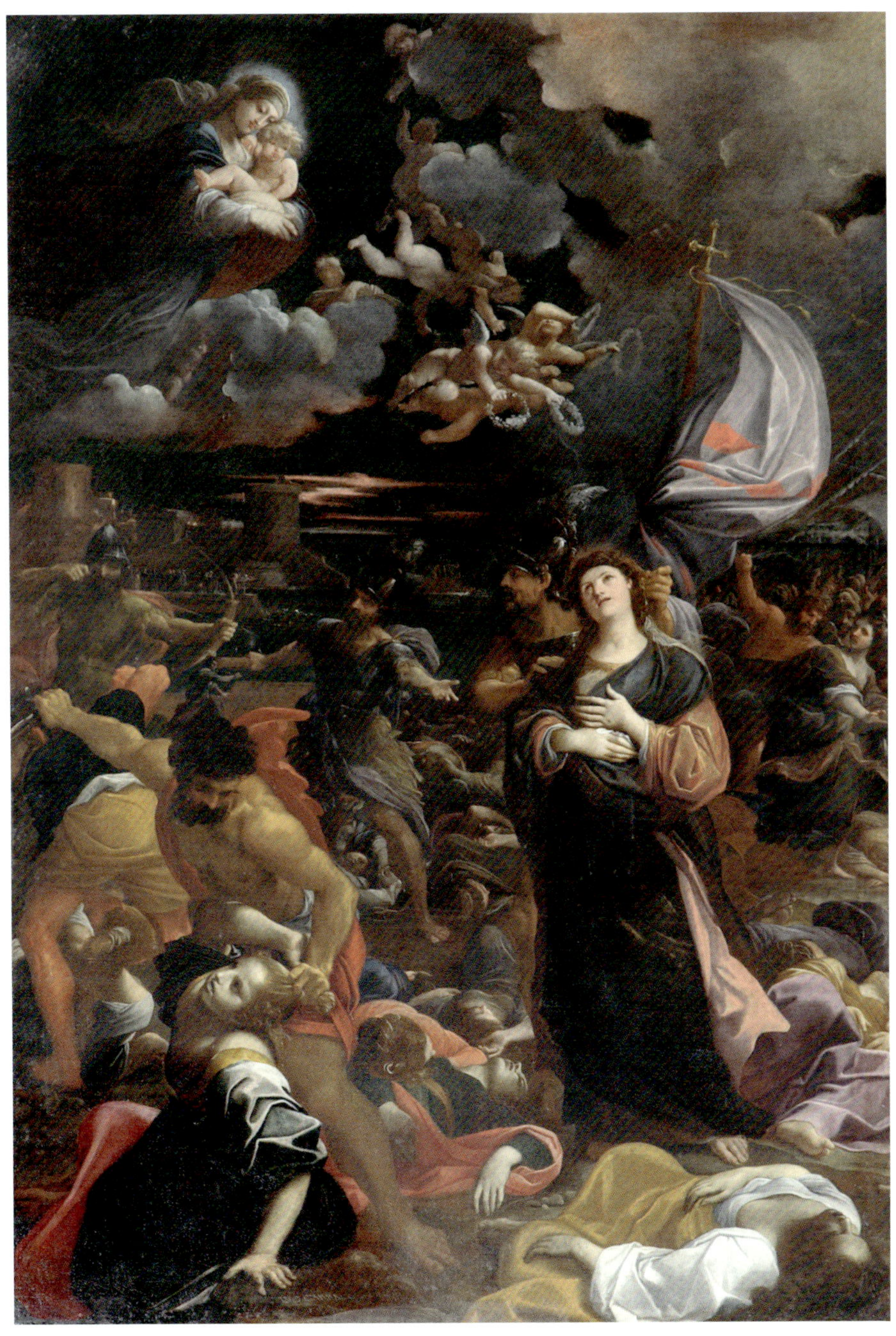

FIG. 33
Vittore Carpaccio (1465–1525)
Martyrdom of the Pilgrims and Funeral of Saint Ursula, from the Ursula cycle, 1495
Oil on canvas, 271 × 561 cm
Gallerie dell'Accademia, Venice

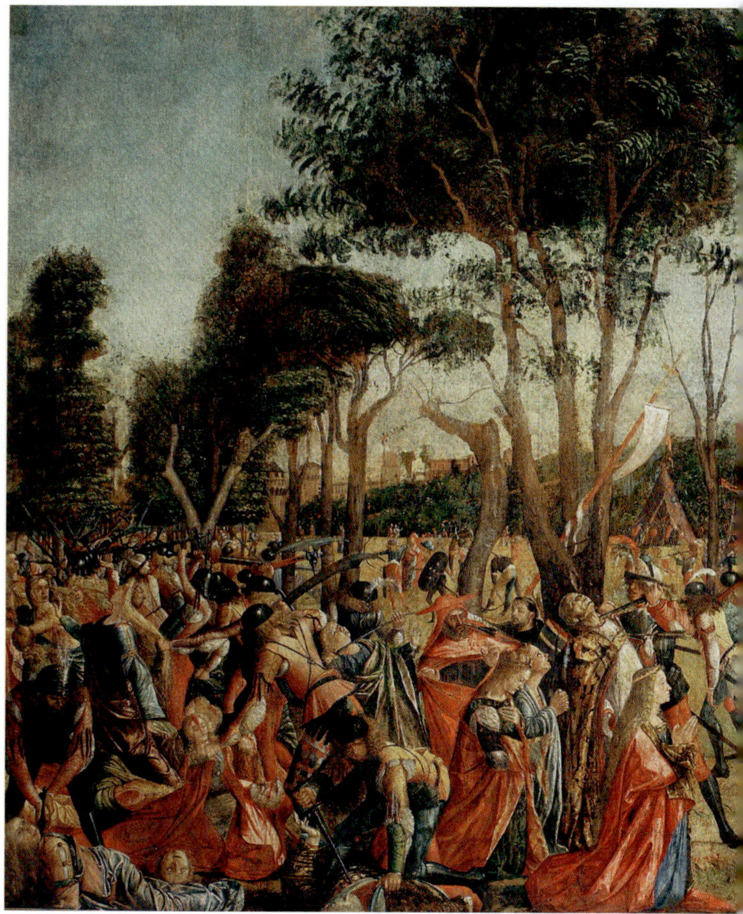

FIG. 34
Early fifteenth-century Ursula shrine from Bruges
Paint on wood,
19 × 32 × 16.3 cm
Groeningemuseum, Stedelijke Musea Brugge

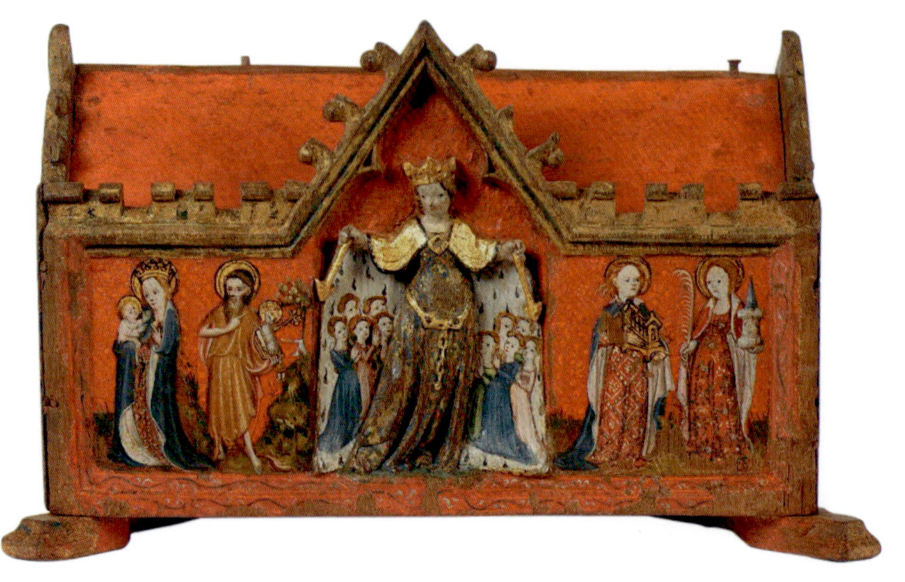

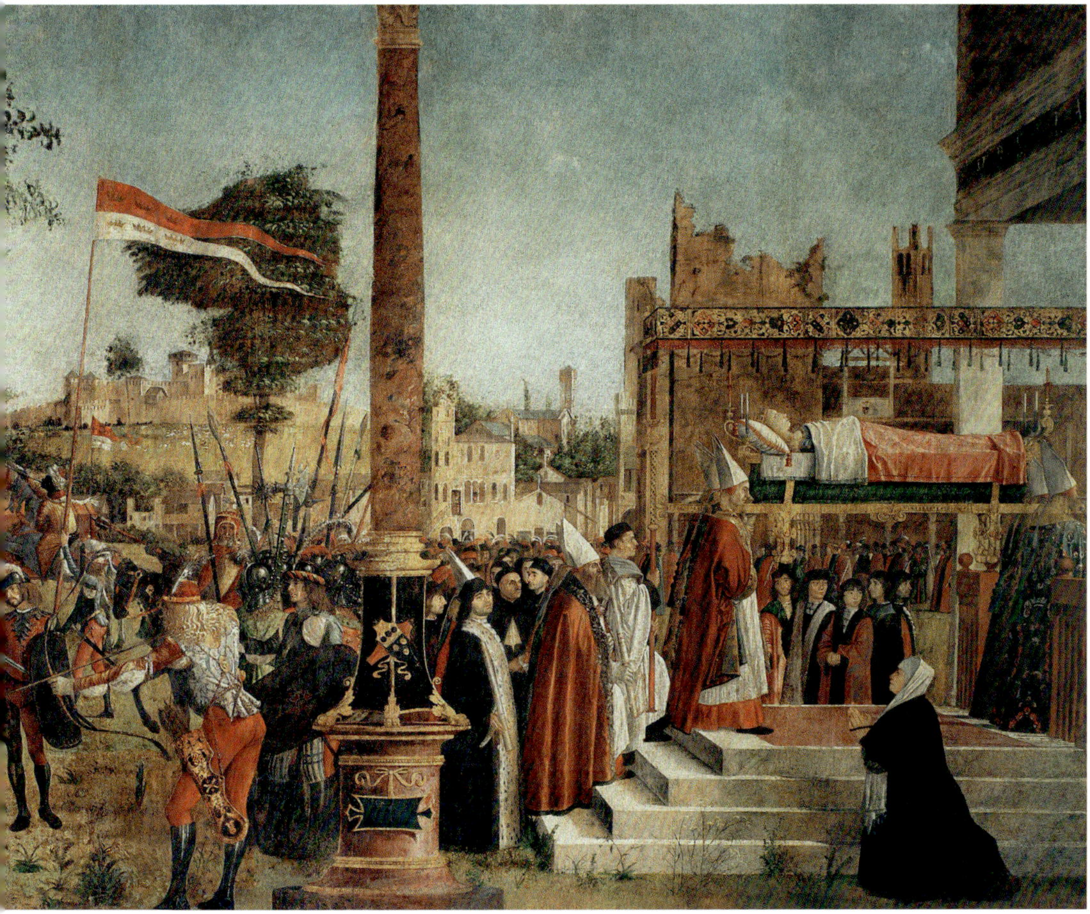

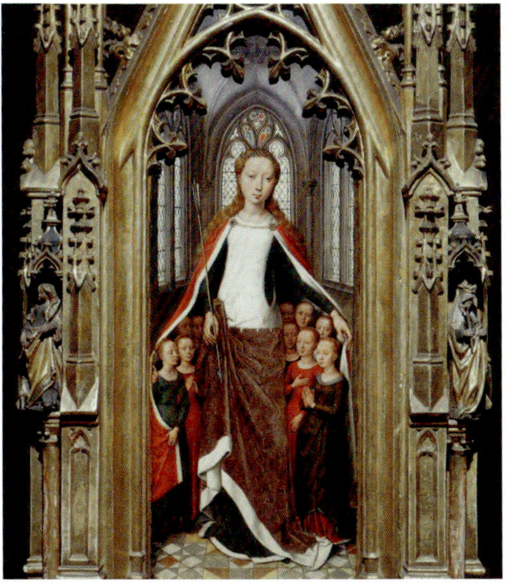

FIG. 35
Hans Memling (active 1465; died 1494)
Saint Ursula sheltering her Virgins, from the Reliquary Shrine of Saint Ursula, 1482
Oil and gilding on panel, 91.5 × 99 × 41.5 cm
Memling Museum, Bruges

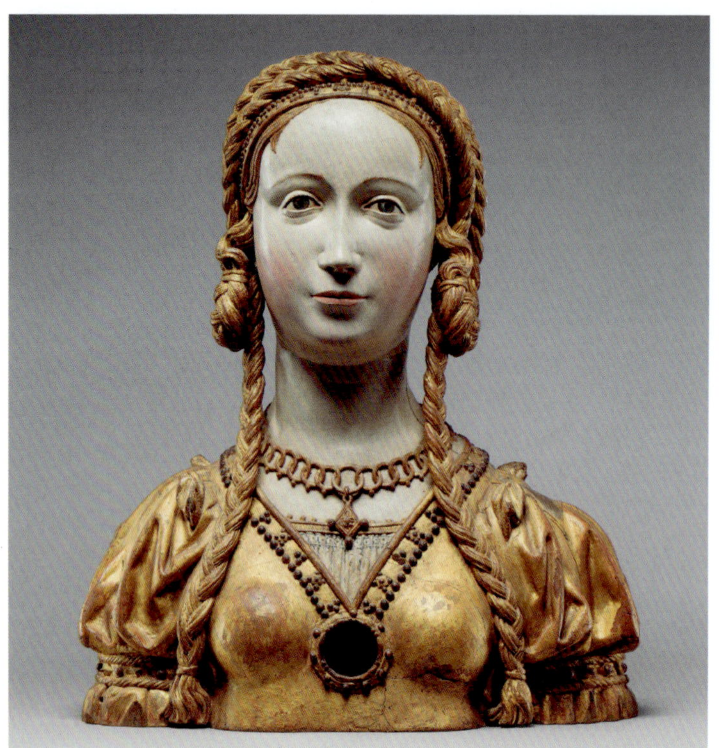

FIG. 36
Reliquary bust of a companion of Saint Ursula, about 1520–30
Oak polychromed and gilt on plaster ground; glass opening for relic, 45.4 cm (height)
The Metropolitan Museum of Art, New York, Gift of J. Pierpont Morgan, 1917

FIG. 37
Golden Chamber of the Basilica of St Ursula, Cologne, decorated with bones believed to belong to the virgin martyrs

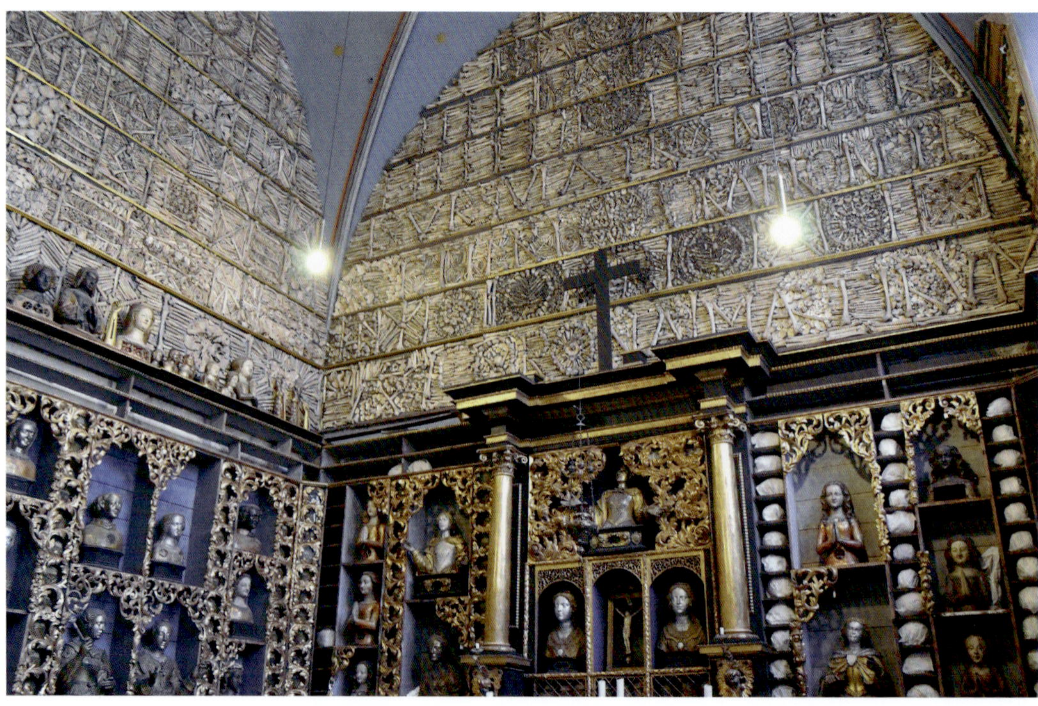